CASE STUDIES IN CULTURAL ANTHROPOLOGY

GENERAL EDITORS

George and Louise Spindler

STANFORD UNIVERSITY

BEING A PALAUAN

JAPAN

OKINAWA

IWO JIMA

PHILIPPINES

ROTA
GUAM

ULITHI

YAP

NGULU

PALAU
ISLANDS

IFALUK

PULAP TRUK

HALMAHERA

MANUS

NEW GUINEA

Being a
PALAUAN

FIELDWORK EDITION

BY

H. G. BARNETT

University of Oregon

HOLT, RINEHART AND WINSTON

NEW YORK   CHICAGO   SAN FRANCISCO   DALLAS
MONTREAL   TORONTO   LONDON   SYDNEY

Library of Congress Cataloging in Publication Data

Barnett, Homer Garner, 1906–
    Being a Palauan.

   (Case studies in cultural anthropology)
   Bibliography: p. 117
   1.   Palau Islands—Social life and customs.
I.   Title.   II.   Series.
DU780.B28   1979   301.29′96′6   78–16350
ISBN: 0–03–045366–6

Foreword

About the Series

These case studies in cultural anthropology are designed to bring to students, in beginning and intermediate courses in the social sciences, insights into the richness and complexity of human life as it is lived in different ways and in different places. They are written by men and women who have lived in the societies they write about and who are professionally trained as observers and interpreters of human behavior. The authors are also teachers, and in writing their books they have kept the students who will read them foremost in their minds. It is our belief that when an understanding of ways of life very different from one's own is gained, abstractions and generalizations about social structure, cultural values, subsistence techniques, and the other universal categories of human social behavior become meaningful.

About the Author

H. G. Barnett has long had a special interest in the Pacific Islands. He has lived in a Palauan village, and he has visited Fiji and New Caledonia, and the then Netherlands New Guinea. As staff anthropologist for the U. S. Government's Trust Territory of the Pacific Islands, he visited all the major island groups of American Micronesia, with extended revisits to Palau to deal with special problems arising from Palauan adaptations to changing conditions. He was also an adviser to the Netherlands New Guinea government on its native welfare programs, and a member of the Research Council of the South Pacific Commission, a body of social scientists which recommended studies of native and administrative needs as traditional patterns were modified through contact with alien cultures and demands. He is Professor Emeritus 'of Anthropology at the University of Oregon, where he has been since 1939. His books include *Palauan Society, Innovation, Anthropology in Administration, Indian Shakers,* and *The Coast Salish of British Columbia,* among others. More information on Dr. Barnett is furnished in the introduction to Chapter 13, "Palauan Journal."

v

About the Book

Palauan men praise women and state with pride, "Women are strong; men are weak." But men do the planning and make the decisions. This is no more strange to a Palauan than the fact that many children whose biological parents are still alive are adopted many times, and that material advantage should accrue from these transactions to several kinsmen of the child.

Dr. Barnett lets readers discover the answers to such seeming puzzles by taking them to the scene. Through the author's inductive approach—a particularly appropriate one for a culture case study—Palauan life and behavior, and the reasons behind that behavior, unfold before the reader.

Besides furnishing an inductive analysis of life on Palau in the present, Dr. Barnett puts that present into perspective on the basis of the past. The effects of successive domination by the Japanese, the Germans, and the Americans, and of new economic wants created by Western goods, are described. Indeed, past and present are woven together so skillfully by the author that the reader, without being presented with a highly formal analysis, is led to a clear conception of important processes of culture change and adaptation.

Fieldwork Edition

This new edition of *Being a Palauan* has been enhanced by the inclusion of a chapter on Homer Barnett's fieldwork in Palau under the title "Palauan Journal," from *Being an Anthropologist: Fieldwork in Eleven Cultures*, edited by G. Spindler. This chapter was written for the express purpose of providing background for this case study. As teachers of introductory anthropology, we find it essential to provide such background. Without an understanding of the fieldwork behind an ethnography, one's understanding of anthropology, and of the specific ethnography, is deficient. Homer Barnett has chosen to communicate what he did, how he did it, and how he felt about it, in the form of a journal of fieldwork activities from day to day over a period of several months. By doing this, he has approximated the actual unfolding of events and relationships that constitute fieldwork as the ethnographer's understanding of the community or group in which he or she is working enlarges and deepens. Though the fieldwork chapter is placed at the end of the case study so as to avoid disrupting the beginning or flow of the text, it can be read profitably before beginning the case study as well as afterwards. Read in any sequence, the case study and the fieldwork chapter make complementary companions.

GEORGE AND LOUISE SPINDLER
General Editors

Calistoga, California
1978

Contents

Strips of thatching are made of nipa palm leaves that are folded over bamboo slats and sewed with banana-stalk fiber.

Carrying on the Palauan tradition of community service, these men are contributing their labor to the construction of a meeting house using modern materials.

Façade of Community Center with adaptations of motifs on men's club houses.

Introduction

THE PALAUS are one of several clusters of islands in that part of the
Pacific Ocean known to anthropologists as Micronesia. They lie about
seven degrees north of the equator, approximately 600 miles east of
Mandanao in the Philippines and about the same distance north of the nearest
point in New Guinea. There are many islands in the Palau group but all are
small; their total land area is only 188 square miles. The largest island, Babeldaob, is twenty miles long and about half that in width. Adjacent to it is
Koror, which has been the administrative center ever since the Palauans have
been under foreign control.

Babeldaob is volcanic in origin. It has rolling hills that reach an eleva-
tion of 700 feet, many small streams, and a partially forested interior. Most
of the other islands are composed of coral limestone, some too rugged to
invite occupation. A reef fringes the land masses. The water of the lagoon
inside it is relatively shallow and quiet; the reef bank drops off sharply to
ocean depths on its seaward side.

The islands have a tropical oceanic climate. Their location within the
tropics prevents the temperature from dropping below 75 degrees, and the
moderating effect of breezes blowing across vast expanses of ocean keeps it
from rising above 85 degrees. The humidity is high and it is this that brings
discomfort to the unacclimated person. The day and night variation in temperature and humidity and their seasonal swings are slight. During the coolest
months, from January to March, a blanket is welcome at night, as it is at
any time during a typhoon. The January to March season is the time of the
trade winds. They blow almost constantly during that period, bringing fair
weather and an opportunity to carry on many activities out-of-doors. Throughout the rest of the year rainfall is constant and heavy, occurring mostly as
afternoon downpours. Precipitation is heaviest during the monsoon season
of July to September when storms blow in from the southwest. The mean
annual rainfall is 156 inches. Typhoons may develop at any time, but they
are most likely to occur between July and November. Many of them sweep
to the north of the Palaus on their westward course, but scarcely a year
passes that does not bring at least one of these destructive storms that far
south.

1

Hardwood trees, used for timber, are found only in certain areas in the interior, as are patches of pandanus and other useful trees, bushes, and vines. Much of the upland is barren, sometimes supporting only a coarse grass. Wild life is scanty and for the most part economically valueless. The only mammals are bats and rats, neither of which is used for food. There are many birds, and chickens and pigeons are hunted.

There are slightly more than 6,000 Palauans. Both physically and culturally they reflect their geographic position. In appearance, many of them, with their long, wavy hair and slight physique, resemble the Indonesians to the west. Others have pronounced Negroid characteristics and so resemble the people of New Guinea to the south. Still others are tall, light skinned, and corpulent like many Polynesians to the east. Presumably they represent an ancient mixture of the Caucasoid, Mongoloid, and Negroid races, with more recent crossings between strains of this ancestral stock. Their language belongs to the far-flung Malayo-Polynesian family, which extends from Madagascar to Easter Island, but it is a distinct branch of this family. There are elements in it which resemble those of some of the Indonesian tongues, and still others with affiliations in Melanesia. It is a very complex language in the sense that it has many irregularities which make the formulation of grammatical and lexical rules difficult. In this respect it resembles English, and the reason may be the same—that is, the assimilation of diverse alien forms of speech. The language of the Palauans is not understood by the Yapese, their nearest neighbors.

The Palaus were discovered by the Spanish in 1543, but little attention was paid to them for many years. Several English traders visited the islands during the eighteenth century. Nominally the islands were a Spanish possession, but that country took no steps to exercise control until 1885. Even then, however, the control was minimal and its effects short lived, for following the Spanish-American War Spain sold her interests in the Pacific to Germany. Whereas the former owners were mostly concerned with missionizing the islands, the new proprietors were intent on their economic exploitation. German influence lasted only a short time, for in 1914 the Japanese seized Germany's holdings in Micronesia and retained them until their surrender to the Americans in 1944-45. Japan had an economic stake in its Pacific possessions and encouraged their colonization by its nationals. Because of this there were at one time nearly 24,000 Japanese in Palau alone. From 1945 to 1951 the area was under the jurisdiction of the U. S. Navy, at first under military controls, later under a civilian government code. At present it is administered by the Interior Department under a trusteeship agreement with the United Nations. Officially it is known as the U. S. Trust Territory of the Pacific Islands, and by the terms of its charter the U. S. Government is obligated to promote the welfare of the islanders under the surveillance of the United Nations Trusteeship Council. There are no Americans in the Territory except those connected with the administration.

The account which follows is based on observations made by the author over a ten-year period. For nine months in 1947-48 he and another anthropologist lived in a village on Babeldaob learning the language and making a record of on-going events. He returned for several less extended visits during 1951-53. In 1958 he again had opportunity to contact several Palauans, though not in Palau itself.

The foundation data to be presented are from the 1947-48 period. Where appropriate they have been modified to make them as nearly contemporary as possible. An effort has been made throughout to convey an understanding of Palauan society and culture by presenting the Palauan view of the world in terms of the author's understanding of how the Palauan sees and comprehends what goes on around him. The objective, then, has been to delineate a way of life as free from the anthropologist's conventionalized structuring of it as possible, in the hope of communicating what it means to live and die in a small village in Palau.

Growing Up

FIVE-YEAR-OLD Azu trails after his mother as she walks along the village path, whimpering and tugging at her skirt. He wants to be carried, and he tells her so, loudly and demandingly, "Stop! Stop! Hold me!" His mother shows no sign of attention. She continues her steady barefooted stride, her arms swinging freely at her sides, her heavy hips rolling to smooth the jog of her walk and steady the basket of wet clothes she carries on her head. She has been to the washing pool and her burden keeps her neck stiff, but this is not why she looks impassively ahead and pretends not to notice her son. Often before she has carried him on her back and an even heavier load on her head. But today she has resolved not to submit to his plea, for it is time for him to begin to grow up.

Azu is not aware that the decision has been made. Understandably, he supposes that his mother is just cross, as she often has been in the past, and that his cries will soon take effect. He persists in his demand, but falls behind as his mother firmly marches on. He runs to catch up and angrily yanks at her hand. She shakes him off without speaking to him or looking at him. Enraged, he drops solidly on the ground and begins to scream. He gives a startled look when this produces no response, then rolls over on his stomach and begins to writhe, sob, and yell. He beats the earth with his fists and kicks it with his toes. This hurts and makes him furious, the more so since it has not caused his mother to notice him. He scrambles to his feet and scampers after her, his nose running, tears coursing through the dirt on his cheeks. When almost on her heel he yells and, getting no response, drops to the ground.

By this time his frustration is complete. In a rage he grovels in the red dirt, digging his toes into it, throwing it around him and on himself. He smears it on his face, grinding it in with his clenched fists. He squirms on his side, his feet turning his body through an arc on the pivot of one shoulder.

A man and his wife are approaching, the husband in the lead, he with a short-handled adz resting on his left shoulder, she with a basket of husked coconuts on her head. As they come abreast of Azu's mother the man greets her with "You have been to the washing pool?" It is the Palauan equivalent of the American "How are you?"—a question that is not an inquiry but a token of recognition. The two women scarcely glance up as they pass. They have recognized each other from a distance and it is not necessary to repeat the greeting. Even less notice is called for as the couple pass Azu sprawled on the path a few yards behind his mother. They have to step around his frenzied body, but no other recognition is taken of him, no word is spoken to him or to each other. There is no need to comment. His tantrum is not an unusual sight, especially among boys of his age or a little older. There is nothing to say to him or about him.

In the yard of a house just off the path, two girls, a little older than Azu, stop their play to investigate. Cautiously and silently they venture in Azu's direction. His mother is still in sight, but she disappears suddenly as she turns off the path into her yard without looking back. The girls stand some distance away, observing Azu's gyrations with solemn eyes. Then they turn and go back to their doorway, where they stand, still watching him but saying nothing. Azu is left alone, but it takes several minutes for him to realize that this is the way it is to be. Gradually his fit subsides and he lies sprawled and whimpering on the path.

Finally he pushes himself to his feet and starts home, still sobbing and wiping his eyes with his fists. As he trudges into the yard he can hear his mother shouting at his sister, telling her not to step over the baby. Another sister is sweeping the earth beneath the floor of the house with a coconut-leaf broom. Glancing up, she calls shrilly to Azu, asking him where he has been. He does not reply, but climbs the two steps to the threshold of the doorway and makes his way to a mat in the corner of the house. There he lies quietly until he falls asleep.

This has been Azu's first painful lesson in growing up. There will be many more unless he soon understands and accepts the Palauan attitude that emotional attachments are cruel and treacherous entanglements, and that it is better not to cultivate them in the first place than to have them disrupted and disclaimed. Usually the lesson has to be repeated in many connections before its general truth sinks in. There will be refusals of pleas to be held, to be carried, to be fed, to be cuddled, and to be amused; and for a time at least there will follow the same violent struggle to maintain control that failed to help Azu. Sometimes mothers will stoically hold their ground, as his mother did, sometimes they will become exasperated and switch the legs of their children with a tough vine, or toss them into the shallow water of the lagoon. More often, in the beginning, they will relent and attempt to console the children whom they have come to love even though they know it will hurt more in the long run. For whatever the means, and regardless of the lapses from the stern code, children must grow away from their parents, not cleave to them. Soon or late the child must learn not to expect the solicitude, the indulgence, and the warm attachment of earlier years and must accept the fact that he is to live in an emotional vacuum, trading friendship for concrete rewards, neither giving nor accepting lasting affection.

As with all people and all lessons, some Palauans learn this one with less turmoil and rebellion than do others. Girls come to know it more gradually than boys, but for both its full meaning dawns with a shock. One reason is that, for boys at least, it represents a reversal in parental attitudes; another is because it is presented so sharply and unexpectedly. Watchful guidance and tenderness is suddenly replaced by parental detachment and querulous impatience, particularly on the part of mothers. Instead of gradually relaxing their concern for their children, they rather abruptly turn away from them and make them take care of themselves; instead of carrying them everywhere, they make them walk; instead of answering to their cry, they go about their business and ignore the child's vigorous protests. At about this time, too, they begin to shout at their children and attempt to apply the ineffective disciplinary device of speaking harshly to them. Chiding replaces indulgence. Parents laugh at their youngsters with others, teasing them about their bodies or about their wants or about their crying.

These gestures of rejection do not mean that the child is abandoned to his own resources at the artless age of five. He is still shielded, guided, and provided for in every physical sense. He is permitted to do many things that will not be permitted to him as an adult. He is even pampered and comforted, but these continued indulgences are under the impersonal ministration of an older sibling or foster sibling, usually a girl. This substitute mother is never quite the same, and very likely no one will ever be, for the child's confidence in himself and in his parents has been shaken. His wishes once had a magical effect. Now the big adult world where things get done has become an uncontrollable mystery. The six- or seven-year-old child no longer knows how to manipulate it, and he is more often told than asked what he wants.

Up until this time few restraints are placed on children. Boys go without clothing entirely; girls are covered about the age of three with a loose dress. Both sexes relieve themselves where the urge comes upon them, around the yard or on the village path. Mothers scold them and shake them, then patiently clean up the mess. Children rest and snack throughout the day and night as they feel the need. They go to bed at dark or stay up until midnight, dozing in the laps of their late-talking parents and falling asleep in odd places and curious positions throughout the day. They wander around the village alone or play in the lagoon, but never stray far from home. One or two of them will usually be found playing around the spot where their fathers are working or gossiping. They are seldom punished but are often scolded in a frightening tone—frightening until they learn that it is not so bad after all, for usually nothing comes of their parents' annoyance.

There is always someone with a little child who serves as protector, provider, and companion. And for the very young there is another ingredient in the compound of attention: love in the person of a mother. She is never far from her infant and she lavishes her free time on it. She nurses it, cleans it, tickles it, makes faces at it, fondly shapes its nose as she would like to see it.

She gives inner warmth to it through sharing herself with it and security through her attentiveness and bodily contact. When she must leave it, as she does almost daily to work in her gardens, it is placed in the care of an older sibling or its father.

Toddlers are the most demanding. They expect and receive constant attention, and it is almost always bestowed with gentleness. They are carried astride the hips of their mothers or sisters who often go visiting in the late afternoon or simply stroll along the village path. In the mornings there is almost always someone doing something somewhere along the way that is mildly interesting. But even if there is nothing to see, the ride is fun, for it is effortless, safe, and stimulating, and it is gratifying to be able to command it.

Fathers play a minor role in all this child service. They do not assume the responsibility for rearing their children. They are fond of them, but theirs is the affection of a bystander. They want children and are obviously proud of them as they grow out of helplessness. They are conscientious providers. They are gentle and patient with the very young. They amuse them and are amused by them. They often tend them when their wives are working and there is no older sister in the household, or during that part of the day when the girls are in school. Yet none of this is the man's job. They involve themselves only when and to the degree that it pleases them. Feeding, bathing, pacifying, and loving—these are for women. The male attitude is something like the zoo visitor: young animals, almost any little living thing, evokes yearning and compassion. As it grows older it loses this appeal and becomes just another animal, sometimes an ugly one. In any event, it is not the spectator's responsibility.

The progress toward womanhood is more modulated and serene than that toward manhood. Girls receive no special consideration from their fathers and they, like their brothers, are cut loose from their mothers early in life. But the emotional severance is less abrupt, for it is a gradual process with no clear beginning. Consequently there are fewer violent reactions to their mothers' withdrawal, fewer verbal clashes, fewer tantrums. Indeed, displays of temper are assumed to be a male prerogative. A tighter rein is held on girls from the beginning. More work is expected of them, hence there is more to keep their minds off themselves. They get less attention, have fewer whims. They grow away rather than being thrust away from their parents, but the end product is the same: an emotionally stranded pre-adolescent whose fathers and mothers are people to whom respect, obedience, and labor are due.

It is well that parenthood is understood in these objective terms, for there is always the possibility that real parents will be replaced by foster parents who expect the same expressions of filial devotion. Adoption is a very common practice. It can happen any time after a child is free of its mother's loving care and can happen more than once to the same person. There are Palauan men who have been adopted after they were married; some have taken the initiative themselves. Many families include natural children as well as one or two who have been adopted.

The United States government requires all children, age 8 and over, to attend the district schools. Some do not enter until later, and there is no attempt to enforce the regulation to the letter. Nevertheless, most children go to school most of the time during the school year, despite the fact that many have to walk well over a mile from their homes. The Japanese instituted schooling in the islands and were much stricter in discipline and attendance requirements and much narrower in their curriculum conception than the Americans. Under their regime all children went to school for three years and a selected few for two years more; even fewer went on for limited vocational training at the capital town of Koror. The Americans emphasize mass education and attempt to put all students through at least the sixth grade. Progress is slow, for there are few textbooks in the Palauan language and the village teachers, who are only beginning to speak English, lack materials upon which to draw for their own learning.

Boys and girls attend the same classes in a war-damaged building with a tin roof, open sides, and rude benches and desks. Following the Japanese pattern, classroom etiquette is rigid, but when the dismissal bell sounds, all formality is dropped. Children leap out of classrooms to play a variety of games during recesses. After school, too, and on holidays the playground is the favorite rendezvous for children of all ages seeking companionship or play. All group games are either Japanese or American. Most of them are competitive, and this includes everything from jacks to baseball.

Palauan games and amusements usually take children away from the school grounds singly or in small groups. Boys hunt pigeons with a blow gun somewhat shorter than man-size. Some of them snare small wild chickens that they keep as pets staked out on a string until the birds languish and die. Both boys and girls capture butterflies with a net made of strong strands of spiders' webs laced around a fork at the end of a wispy reed. Musical toys include cane flutes and blades of grass stretched between the thumbs; both produce recognizable tunes. These amusements, and many more, are short-lived fads. They are revived every year, each one according to its season, as marbles and kites are with us.

School-aged girls have domestic duties that are not heavy but are routine and dull. They tend their younger brothers and sisters, wash clothes, and clean the house; they collect bits of driftwood and dried coconut-leaf sheaths to be used as firewood. It is their job to keep their yards clean by sweeping them with a long bundle of coconut-leaf midribs. Most of the yards are dotted with clumps of flowering plants, the care of which is also a girl's assignment. They help their mothers plant sweet potatoes near the house, and on occasion assist them in the taro fields. Not until they become marriageable do they undertake women's work in earnest, planting and gathering taro roots in the black knee-deep mud where the plant must be grown.

Little girls do not play with dolls; neither do they "play house." They are not encouraged to express themselves through these make-believe substitutes for real life, and it seems not to occur to them spontaneously. Now and then one or two will be seen wearing lipstick, earrings, and old dresses much too big for them. They give the impression, though, that playing at being grown-up does not appeal to them. It may be that they feel themselves to be strangers to an adult life that is too remote and confusing to invite invitation.

This seems also to be the case with boys. In comparison with their sisters, they have little to do—nothing that is essential, at least—until they are fourteen or fifteen. As soon as they can handle a fish spear or a net they trail their fathers into the lagoon or go by themselves as the fancy strikes them. They punt rafts, paddle outrigger canoes, and learn to skin dive on their own. Men do not introduce their sons to the sea, the economic domain of the Palauan male, nor do they urge and coach them toward an eventual mastery of it. They prefer other men for fishing companions and pay little attention to the boys who straggle along observing and learning as the opportunity offers. It is the same with the making of a net, or the carving of a bowl, or the construction of a house. If a boy wants to learn these things, he goes to a man who is especially competent in them. Equally crucial is the failure of the older men gradually to expose and explain to their sons the intricacies of Palauan political scheming, prestige competition, and social controls. All that the maturing youth can do is watch and listen, and sometimes ask questions. He soon learns, however, that there are taboo areas, whole sectors of life that are so completely closed to him that even self-instruction is impossible.

There is thus a definite rift between the generations, and it is further emphasized in still other ways. In ancient times, the gap was institutionalized by the formation of clubs comprised of age mates of the same sex. When boys and girls reached the age of 14 or 15, they were automatically inducted into a formal organization composed of their peers. Up to this point there were play groups, friendships, work groups, and other associations based on personal preference, convenience, or domestic necessity. Entering a club was quite a different matter. It was required by tradition and it entailed many obligations, the most important of which was community service.

Age dominated youth in club life as outside it. It also dictated different sets of interests and personal affiliations. Old men, middle-aged men, and youths had their separate duties, rights, and loyalties. The same was true of women, who belonged to parallel organizations. As a result there were formal requirements which divided not only male from female but child from parent and grandparent. With adolescence there came a further drawing apart of the domestic constellation of father, son, mother, and daughter, leaving less to share than there was previously.

Club life as such has ceased to exist, and today only its community service aspect remains. The favorable aspects of its passing, however, are at present being offset by the estrangement produced by education. School children are being taught things unheard of by their elders, sometimes in direct contradiction to traditional values and understandings. Directly or by implication they are told that the old people are relics of the past, honest and sincere, but unfortunately ignorant and superstitious. Their ways are childish, their views misguided. Quite literally, young people are today learning to speak a different language from that of their parents, some of whom know Japanese, some only Palauan, very few English. Even relatively young parents who were partly assimilated into Japanese life are becoming intellectual strangers to their Americanized children.

From the growing-up process there thus emerges a Palauan youth who has learned to take things as they come without much questioning. He is reserved, pragmatic, tentative; if something works, it is good, but one can never be sure. On the threshold of adulthood he possesses the virtues of a citizen who knows how to keep his place. He is obedient to authority, deferential before age and rank. He has learned not to stick his neck out very far, not to venture, for life is full of uncertainties and one only invites trouble by assuming the responsibilities appropriate to someone else. He has learned to subordinate his interests to those of the community on demand and to keep out of sight, when he can, if he is to avoid requisitions on his time and privacy.

What he has not learned is how to be an adult, for growing up in Palau is a discontinuous process. Certainly for boys, and to some extent for girls, it has two major breaks and many minor jolts. Growing up is not a process of integrating present experience with either the past or the future. It is demanding and goading but does not provide the means for functioning as a full-fledged member of society. There is no preparation for taking the important step into adulthood, and many never take it, either socially or psychologically. To others, if not to themselves, these socially stunted individuals remain children even though they may have grandchildren of their own.

2

Facing the World

OR THE PALAUAN, most of the world is outside him. It is made up of things, people, and events that move, as he does, because something else moves; not because of a spontaneous inner prompting. Feelings, urges, reasons, and purposes exist, but they are inscrutable or indecipherably connected with doing or acting. Man is at the mercy of an impersonal universe of unpredictable—often alarming—events that can be parried and parlayed to personal advantage or adjusted to, but not initiated. It is a rebounding, recoiling universe, an endless succession of external causes, the beginnings of and reasons for which no man can fathom. All that he knows is that something happens to him. Then he acts; not before. Man does not control his destiny. He adapts himself to pressures and diverts them along to others. He is a channel for action, a receiver and a transmitter, not an originator. The wise man, the effective man, is a pragmatist. He deals with situations in their concrete reality and with things as his senses convey them; his behavior follows established patterns, and he does not venture on unexplored ground. He faces "facts" and does not worry much about trying to explain them.

This positivistic approach to life situations is evident in Palauan reactions to TAT (Thematic Apperception Test) cards. A sample of subjects representing a cross section of Palauan society were shown a series of cards on each of which was pictured a rather ambiguous scene. The people and things in the scenes were sketchily portrayed and interrelated in uncertain ways or juxtaposed for unstated reasons. The ambiguity of such pictures is central to the purpose of the investigation, which is to prompt the observer to tell a story about what is happening in each picture. Inevitably the subject reads in meanings and interpretations which tell more about him psychologically than they do about the pictures. He "projects" himself, and thereby unwittingly discloses his understanding of the world.

For the Palauan story teller, things happen to the people on the TAT cards abruptly; the people come to life for a short time—the stories are always very short and unelaborated—they act mechanically, and then run down, the stimulus having spent itself. Frequently, in order to account for what seems to be taking place the story teller will introduce a cause for which there is no pictorial clue, something "picked out of thin air," to start the action. The pictures evoke brief, matter-of-fact interpretations that do not go much beyond what can actually be seen. The stories are literal, concrete, and "picture dominated." To the extent that visual clues are few, the stories are sketchy and unfleshed, and they sometimes stop abruptly short of any speculation. One card, for example, shows a person (presumably a man) kneeling beside a canoe with his back to the viewer and his face in his hands. A frequent response to this scene was, "This person has his back to me so I don't know what he is doing."

Feeling so much at the mercy of enigmatic forces external to himself, a Palauan is quite sensitive to what the psychologist calls "press." The press or pressure sensed by the Palauan comes mainly from two sources, the natural environment and people of authority. Each of these sources of power has its benign and its threatening aspects; that is, each can be sensed as supportive and comforting or as harmful and upsetting. Any occurrence out of the ordinary is likely to be startling or momentarily shocking. Pictures of a disturbed environment are quite often disturbing to Palauan viewers: a TAT scene of a thatched house surrounded by palm trees bending under a heavy wind, a deserted beach with a ruined house, a broken canoe, and something that might be taken to be a part of a human skeleton—all these are upsetting. Even the expected event can inspire vague feelings of distrust and fear if it is shrouded in uncertainty. This is why the night is fearsome. Doorways are blocked at dark and a dim light burns in every sleeping room. Anciently the light came from a coconut-oil pottery lamp with the wick in its spout; now it is a kerosene lamp or lantern that burns all night.

The whims of authority figures loom prominently as the determinants of behavior. The demands of parents, brothers-in-law, chiefs, husbands, older people, and foreigners are relentless. They are burdensome and leave little opportunity for reflection or independent effort. They can be anticipated but not planned for, scheduled, or moderated, for they emerge from obscure reasons or spring from contingencies such as deaths, births, and battles. In spite of all this, they are comforting, for they relieve one of the responsibility of taking the initiative. They remove the terror of standing alone. They dispel the nightmare of unshared failure.

The dependence upon others and the acceptance of anything this brings is well illustrated by Palauan adjustment to foreign authority. The islands have been controlled and the lives of the people changed by first the Germans, then the Japanese, and now the Americans. The Palauans have not rebeled against their fickle history; their fate as a people has not been too unlike their individual experience in growing up. Foreigners, like fathers, have their own reasons for doing what they do; and they come and go. Unlike their fellow Micronesians, the Ponapeans, the Palauans have never risen against their foreign overlords; unlike their nearest neighbors, the Yapese, they have not stoically and resolutely rejected alien ideas. Philosophically, the more educated Palauans now ask, "Who is next? The Russians?"

This waywardness of human destiny produces an ambivalent attitude toward those who hold the reins of power. For them there is deference and subservience, and an alert and eager willingness to please that is genuine and sincere. Tact, politeness, and reserve are the instruments, and the only instruments, of control; never brashness, brusqueness, or hauteur. But there is a residue of latent hostility which slips out in unguarded moments and through indirect avenues. At times it is focused upon the person who is the cause; sometimes it is displaced and finds its target in some innocent but powerless individual; sometimes it is turned upon the self. Often the hostility is flatulent and easily punctured.

One night the young men of Geklau staged a protest against a headman's alleged right to call upon their village for community labor. Beginning early in the afternoon they set about fortifying their courage with a raw homemade liquor distilled from a mash of tapioca roots. By dark the whole village was in a state of alarm over their rowdyism, which increased as time went on. Alarm developed into terror when they began to fire shots in the air and brandish long bush knives at each other and in the doorways of nearby houses. Women and children huddled, screamed, and ran to other houses. Sensing what was coming, most men who did not want to become involved had earlier faded away to visit with friends in adjacent villages. A few older ones sat in the darkened corners of their homes anxiously waiting for the demonstrators to exhaust themselves and their bluster. They knew that the potvaliance was mostly harmless swagger that imperiled no one for all its apparent ferocity, and that it would have wilted under a firm hand.

The most frequent expressions of hostility are disguised behind the façade of pleasantries which Palauans present in their interpersonal dealings. They are a witty people and they enjoy jokes on each other and on themselves. In any culture, some humor is cruel, but by American standards Palauans are shockingly callous. They evoke amusement not only by spotlighting ineptitude and stupidity, but also personal defects, blemishes, and painful misfortunes.

Threatening acts and open antagonisms are rare at present. Hostile feelings are for the most part repressed and can be discovered only through their symbolic expressions such as occur in joking and in reactions to Rorschach ink blots. This personality test consists of splashes of ink, colored or black and gray, which a subject is asked to describe, and like apperceptive story telling, responses to them are self-revealing. Palauan reactions to a standardized series of Rorschach tests support the impression that the Palauan emotional gamut is lopsided. The sanguine emotions of love, delight, hope, and yearning are shallow and constricted, outbalanced in intensity by resentment, alarm, suspicion, embarrassment, anger, shock, and surprise. Reactions to the blots also suggest that emotional displays are spasmodic and that when they do take place they are reported with embarrassment. The actor, sensing his childishness, is as upset as is his audience; he has made a spectacle of himself and stands naked before the watchers. The analysis of Rorschach responses also indicates the absence of introspection and consequently a lack of motivational insight—a bewilderment as to why people do what they do. Action is reaction, not a manifestation of desire. Since spontaneity is so incomprehensible, it is much more comfortable to meet and deal with others on a formal, well-regulated plane, guided by a traditional protocol.

One cannot afford to have much of an emotional investment in a kaleidoscopic universe where everything depends on unknown forces external to one's self. Its shifting constellations of things and people would be too harrying for a steadfast attachment or a conviction. Palauans therefore distrust emotional involvement and deny themselves the luxury of its rewards out of fear of its punishment. Women are more vigilant in this respect than men. They are more passive and resigned, less volatile and self-giving. Both sexes from adolescence on are retractive and guarded in their interpersonal contacts.

Intimacy of association offers no clue to blood relationship; neither do manifestations of interest or concern. Seeming strangers to a household turn out to be parents of children living there; a supposed father and son are discovered to be brothers-in-law. Man and wife hold themselves aloof in public; any demonstration of affection or concern is undignified. More specifically, it is unmasculine. The outsider in time discovers one sign of this relationship: a husband addresses his wife in a brusque, imperious tone that dispels any suspicion that he might be fond of her.

As revealed by their TAT responses, Palauans see their mothers as passive drudges, sickly and harassed by the dual demands of child care and hard work. Invariably the mother in a story has work to do and at the same time is trying to supervise her children. It is she who disciplines them, by scolding; it is she who preaches virtues to them, through cautions and rebukes; it is she who solaces them, rewards them, and carries out their father's instructions with respect to them. She is rarely the object of a child's affection or hostility. There is neither warmth nor coldness in his relationship to her; but of all the authority figures envisaged by the Palauans, she is spoken of most kindly and sympathetically. Children feel with her and for her. Resentment of her is infrequent, veiled, and indirect; the feelings of daughters rather than sons are most often colored by it.

Fathers, in the mind's eye of the Palauan, are more complex and enigmatic figures. They are the real sources of domestic authority, but it is usually deflected through the mother. Attitudes toward them are ambivalent, for they are symbols of both indulgence and power. Very likely this ambivalence is a reaction to a composite image of fatherhood, one component of which is the experience of a young, unimportant head of a family who is himself scarcely more than a child, the other that of a mature man too preoccupied with financial and other obligations to be much concerned with children as human beings. In the imagery of TAT responses, men are frequently described as being forever on some business bent. Before departing, they turn their children over to their wives with instructions for their care. They sometimes have to shake off their youngest who wants to go along. Despite more frequently disguised expressions of resentment toward the father, there are evident expressions of a longing to be with him.

The comforting feeling that comes with dependency on such power figures as parents, chiefs, and foreigners also flows from any human association. Palauans dread isolation, not so much physically as socially and psychologically. "Going it alone" has too many pitfalls and renders the individual too vulnerable to unpredictable events. For this reason decisions come hard, for they affix responsibility too definitely and personally. The best thing to do is to postpone or relay their uncomfortable and thankless demands. Eventually, of course, the end of the line is reached and somebody must act. If the consequences of the decision are more than commonplace, the Palauan solution is to share the responsibility for making it. No person, not even the highest ranking chief, decides an issue of importance or announces a policy solely on his own initiative. Men rise and fall together; success and failure are shared experiences.

Palauan anxiety is chronic, but it is normally concealed behind a display of indifference. This superficial calmness can be shaken by some untoward event, such as an accident, or by an ill-considered demonstration of emotion. It shows up consistently in response to Rorschach figures. These responses, moreover, indicate that the tension is deep seated and self-perpetuating. Such anxiety produces a psychological state that might be described as a fear of fear. It is pervasive, free floating, and is likely to attach itself to any situation that is at all unexpected or unfamiliar. It paralyzes the other feeling states and results in a low degree of emotional flow. It apparently stems from a lack of self-acceptance, a rejection of impulses as damaging; and it produces the sensation of being torn by an inner struggle which cannot be faced or expressed. It obstructs action and thought as well as feeling. Its victims are unable to realize their intellectual potential, and they often find themselves "sitting on the fence," unable to make up their minds on an issue, waiting for something to happen to break the deadlock.

Such intrapsychic warfare is not conducive to self-assurance and inner composure. It completely eliminates boasting and ostentatious display. Though Palauans are obsessed with ambition, though they are engrossed with financial dealings to improve their position and power, no one brags, no one diverts attention to himself, no one bluffs. Everyone is humble, poor, and unimportant. The finest food, the most expensive home, the most beautiful mat, the biggest catch of fish—each is acknowledged with deference and apology. All wealth, all striving, and all pride is concealed, called by another name. It is not only that misfortune can humiliate a braggart; few can muster the conviction that makes one. Internal resources are too dissipated by doubt to provide a strong support. Self-confidence, such as it is, comes only with advancing age and the acquisition of wealth. It is on these external supports that a man must rely and it is from them that he draws courage to speak boldly and to act for other men as well as himself.

Imagination is certain to be constrained and innovation curtailed by self-doubts, and the Palauans are not in fact radically creative. They are skillful, and proficiency is considered a virtue. They greatly admire the clever manipulator of things or of men, but not the reformer, the trail blazer, or the speculator. Their novelties are rephrasings of standard themes, like American love songs, or involuted reapplications of the same device, like the committee system. They eschew flights of fancy in their art, and their story telling is a recital of events which end abruptly. They do not spin yarns; their jokes are witticisms, sharp and to the point, not build-ups with a punch line. In describing what they see in TAT pictures, they name what is rather than imagine what might be happening: "That person is Yapese, so I don't know what he is doing."

The assimilation of alien behaviors and ideas is another matter. Throughout their history the Palauans have welcomed innovations introduced from the outside while fearing to make changes from within. Presumably this is because deviations from custom without a working model to copy are isolating and fraught with uncertainty. Foreigners, by their very presence, are worthy of respect, if they have self-respect. They are obviously power laden and ingenious to have created the marvels they treat so casually and to have come to Palau from mysterious places. Moreover they are complacent, confident, and decisive. They are positive, hence their ways must be good. The result of this attitude is that Palauan culture is a fusion of many customs of diverse origins. It is a compound of Trukese, Yapese, English, Spanish, German, Japanese, and American, and we know not what from New Guinea and the Indies.

Along with this receptivity goes a deep sense of inferiority that their treatment by foreigners has reinforced. To some extent all foreigners have contributed to Palauan debasement, but the Japanese were the most explicit and systematic in reinforcing it. They taught school children that they were congenitally inferior to the Japanese and could never hope to match them in spirit or intelligence. True, Palauans are powerful and cunning, but so are animals. The children had no reason to question this doctrine and they were witnesses to its social consequences. Except for the few taken into Japanese homes as servants, they and their parents were treated with contempt. They were not allowed to enter Japanese homes unless, in the exceptional case, they were seated at the threshold on a mat to protect the floor. In mixed groups in public places the Japanese held their noses, objecting to the odor of coconut oil. On boats and buses they were segregated.

The social gulf between the two races made intermarriage virtually impossible, but it did not prevent illicit relations between Japanese men and Palauan women. Similar clandestine affairs continued after the arrival of American servicemen in 1945. In neither instance were the men entirely at fault, for there were Palauan girls who wanted mixed-blood children even if they had to be born out of wedlock. They, and often their families, believed that the advantages of miscegenation offset the stigma of illegitimacy. They were convinced that a part-Japanese or a part-American child was certain in the long run to be intellectually superior to a full-blooded Palauan.

In the early years of American control it was not uncommon to hear Palauans compare themselves with animals. They seemed to revel in debasement as they discussed the subject among themselves, some going so far as to say that they should be put in pens like hogs or tethered with ropes around their necks like cattle. While not advocating such extremes, there were many who freely said that Palauans have no sense and do not know right from wrong; that they talk a lot and say nothing; that the Americans should not ask them what they want but give them orders as the Germans and the Japanese did.

This attitude has impeded the efforts of Americans to instill democratic principles and promote their long-range objective of self-determination for the Palauans. It has been difficult for the Palauans to learn to make decisions for themselves and to assume responsibility for them. Some take American permissiveness as a license for the pursuit of personal pleasure and gain at the expense of their fellows. The rest are bewildered, saying that while other people may know what is best for them, the Palauans do not. They are ignorant. The Americans are enlightened and so should take the responsibility, treating them as parents treat children, kindly but firmly.

Ambition seems out of place in this setting of timidity and self-devaluation. But it is there, so unmistakably a part of Palauan personality as to suggest an integral connection. Observable behavior and response to psychological tests testify to its pressures. Furthermore, both lines of evidence lead to the conviction that the compulsion to excel springs from feelings of inadequacy and that in general its aims surpass the capabilities of the individual laboring under its goad. The drive is "inflated" and unrealistic, and it receives most of its satisfaction in daydreaming and imaginary successes—in short, autistic fantasies. These mental "achievements" are wish fulfilling, but they are not usually constructive and do not lead to actual realization of the wish.

Ambition frequently breeds rivalry, which in Palau is most congenial when it is not announced. It manifests itself in undercover maneuvers for money and power and in the struggle for independence and leadership in the traditional system of esteem and control. Today it is evident in young men's attempts to establish themselves outside this system, particularly in education. Palauans are known throughout the Trust Territory for their determination to surpass each other and the rest of the Micronesians in the schoolroom. In this and in other areas of competition, such as athletics, they find kindred spirits in their guardians and well-wishers, the Americans.

In fact, despite their many differences, the Palauans and the Americans are much alike in disposition. Palauans, young and old, find American leanings toward practicality, self-centered aims, progress, and competition congenial to their own traditionally ingrained preferences. Or, since they are a congenial and charming people who want to be loved, perhaps they just act that way.

3

Giving Women Credit

THE PALAUANS LIVE in a man's world for which they give women credit. "Women are strong, men are weak," they say. In this expression, which is often repeated by men with the glowing approval of their women, they have in mind not so much the physical strength of women—though that is important too—as the pivotal role the women play in consolidating men's power. They are the channels through which wealth and influence flow. They are the *ro'olel a udoth,* the path by which all money moves into the family chest and by which hereditary leadership is transmitted. Moreover, they are not passive links in the social and political network; they augment the family fortunes by their industry and feminine intrigue. What is not mentioned in emphasizing their importance is that it is their brothers, fathers, and uncles who operate the controls of the system and who plan the tactics for its manipulation.

Men are disposed to be quite generous in their acknowledgement of women's worth if the admission does not alter the fundamental reality of male dominance. They will claim for their women, and allow their women to claim for themselves, some very important rights as long as they are exercised discreetly, in moderation, and do not interfere with their own plans. Their magnanimity is genuine. They believe what they say about the importance of women, so much so that they are almost carried away by their gratitude in praising their women to an interested outsider. The men enjoy their candid admissions of indebtedness, and so do the women. They understand each other; but their warm agreement and the proofs they adduce have been known to trap sympathetic but unwary foreigners into believing that the Palauans live under a matriarchal system presided over by respected, kindly, elderly women.

One fact contributing to this misunderstanding is the one that accounts for the channeling of wealth and authority through women. This is the existence of a matrilineal system by the rules of which a child is born into the clan of its mother, not its father. That is, for the purposes of reckoning social responsibilities and privileges on the basis of birth, a person in Palau is affiliated with his mother, her brothers and sisters, and their mother and her siblings, rather than with the corresponding relatives on the father's side. This means of determining kinship exists in other societies as well, and often it has nothing essentially to do with the exercise of authority. In Palau it has not; power and the sex through which it is inherited are distinct. More specifically, men hold and disburse the family wealth, are invested with family titles and the governing prerogatives that go with them, and take precedence privately and publicly over their sisters, mothers, and wives.

To the Palauans, one of the most important meanings of kinship is that it entails financial assistance, and its linkages are points of transfer of valuable goods. Kinsmen linked by female relatives are the collective beneficiaries of real property and money paid to them by the husbands of their sisters, mothers, and grandmothers. These women are thought of as having earned by their labor such income for their husbands. It is said that the money is theirs, as is the patrimony given to their male kinsmen for them by their fathers. Everyone agrees upon this manner of speaking and upon its essential truth. But in Palau, ownership does not, in the case of females, coincide with proprietorship. The latter right, the right of control, resides with male kinsmen; and that claim is not questioned any more than is the claim of ownership. In the disposition of the wealth of their matrilineage, women are consulted about their individual contributions to it. They speak up in family parleys and they may be quite influential behind the scenes. Furthermore they are background witnesses to the transfer of their property in the interest of their lineage or clan. But no man will admit, and no woman in the presence of her male kinsmen will assert, that her earnings or inheritance are hers to bestow.

The issue of proprietorship looms most clearly with respect to taro lands. These are worked solely by women. Because they are so exclusively, and by men's standards happily, a woman's responsibility, the question of their proprietorship poses a delicate problem. Men hesitate to proclaim ownership, for they want none of the obligations of use-right that goes with it. Typically they resolve the dilemma by admitting female proprietorship unless it involves a conflict with their plans. Fortunately for them, such conflicts are rare, for there is always more land than can be drawn into taro cultivation. The issue is mostly a rhetorical one; and women, in the presence of men, usually have the wisdom, gained through long experience, to back down on it.

Women have their own hierarchy of control. German anthropologists who lived with the Palauans in the early years of this century were much impressed by what they called "women's government." They observed then, as it is possible to observe now, the deference that is accorded to dignified old women, secure in their possession of family titles which correspond to the chiefly titles of their brothers and maternal uncles. These titles are inherited in the female line, as are the men's titles, and they carry with them comparable but complementary authority. In other words, they give their possessors a pre-eminence among women and a commanding voice in their deliberations, but they bring with them only the respectful acknowledgment of men, not authority over them. The "women's government" is, in fact, under orders to the chiefs, who are always men. Whether it be the weeding of the village path, the preparation of food for visiting dignitaries, or a dance, the word goes out and the women get to work.

The influence of titled women is pervasive, not only in the realm of female affairs but outside it as well. Men of all ages look up to them as something of a mother image, and no personage in Palau inspires a more sentimental and truly graceful veneration than do they. This is quite apart from the formal expression of esteem to which they are entitled. Indeed, the attitude toward them is extended to any elderly woman who has the same personal qualities. All such women, titled or not, are called *ma'as,* which means simply "old woman" in its more praiseworthy sense.

Because of these attitudes, the views of elderly—and especially, titled—women carry weight with men. On another plane, and for other reasons, the opinions of wives and sisters infuse and sometimes mold the thinking of their husbands and brothers in gross or subtle ways, depending on their personalities, family connections, and a number of other factors affecting intersex relationships. These influences are therefore personal; they are individualized and contingent on circumstances. They constitute an unformalized aspect of culture in the Palau Islands, as elsewhere, but Palauan men, like men elsewhere, are reluctant to admit this. They are women's ways of playing a men's game. They are effective, but do not produce to a matriarchy.

In Palau it is evident that men have the last word, even if they have to resort to physical force to convince their most likely disputant, a wife. Outside the home, in family councils, and in casual congregations of people, women speak up, and they are given respectful attention. If they are elderly matrons they may express themselves quite positively, but when a husband or a man of rank has had enough of their talk he ends it with a sharp pronouncement.

The prominence given to certain female activities is likely to create the impression for an outsider that women are asserting their importance and demanding a place in the public eye. They are, for example, the key figures in all the ceremonial aspects of crisis rites. They play the important roles in the public rituals associated with birth, marriage, and death. After the delivery of a first child, a woman is formally subjected to a five- to ten-day regimen of ritual strengthening presided over by her female relatives. At the end a high-ranking woman is grandly escorted outside her house and re-introduced to the assembled people as a mother. Her new status is then symbolized by a ritual foot washing by her husband's sisters. While this is taking place, the men squat around the edge of the crowd or peer like schoolboys from nearby doorways. At funerals, women with traditionally designated relationships to the deceased station themselves around the corpse as mourners. From time to time during the vigil other women arrive to console the mourners and to show their grief. Again, during this display of female concern the men sit stolidly apart, around the walls of the room or huddled in small groups in the yard, and chat.

On such occasions it is a woman's duty to represent her male kinsmen and testify to their concern in the matter at hand. Women are expected to be grief stricken at death and so they are. Men cannot be so emotionally involved. Indeed, the presence of women in the public part of a ceremony can be regarded not as an acknowledgment of their interest nor as an admission of their indispensability but rather as a duty which requires them to act in ways that are beneath the dignity of the male sex. Women are sad or gay, whether or not they feel such emotion; men remain unmoved regardless of their feelings.

The conventionalization of these roles is most evident at the death of a spouse or a high chief. A widow is inconsolable and even hysterical at the loss of her husband, as are all women at the death of a chief. There is little in the relationship between a man and a wife or between women and their chiefs during life that would presage such feelings of loss. Fortunately for husbands and common men, this fact gives no cause for embarrassment. Their troubles at deaths, births, and marriages are financial, and they resolve them in long, anxious sessions that are physically removed from the events which precipitate them and that have no apparent connection with them.

The social rituals surrounding the crises of life, however, are not considered by the Palauans to be suitable vehicles for the expression of rank; they are simply means of stressing kinship, and women are the keystones in this structure. On occasions where rank does count, women will always be found at some distance from the place of honor. Some may be command performers; the rest will be on the outer fringes of male spectators. When the dances for an interdistrict entertainment are presented, the visiting and resident chiefs sit in a row of chairs just in front of the dancing line. If American officials are present they sit with the chiefs or in front of them. Behind these dignitaries, or on the wings, are the inactive old men. They occupy chairs if there are enough to go around; otherwise they stand. Back of them are women and children of all ages sitting on the floor or standing wherever they can find a place. If the performance is out of doors—which it is when given during the day—women and children gather back of the dancing line or stand some distance away in the shade of buildings or trees. In any case, no provision is made for them to enjoy the festivities. They must see to it that the men are well provided for. Their place, so to speak, is in the kitchen.

This is quite literally so when their husbands have guests, who are always men. Husbands and wives do not go out for dinner. If they are staying with friends or relatives away from home they eat separately, as do their host and hostess. Visiting women eat in the area of the house reserved for cooking, where they serve themselves after their husbands. They do not have luncheon parties, and the Palauan head of a household would be shocked at the suggestion that his wife prepare food for her friends. This is her obligation to him, one that he has bought in marrying her, and he takes care to see that it is reserved for him alone. Here is an American's description of a noon-time meal with Dois, the second chief of one of the northern districts of Babeldaob:

Today Dois took me to his house for lunch and "a little talk"—and I think as a repayment for a can of tobacco that I gave to him. We arrived about 11:30 and ate at 1:00, his wife starting to cook at his request as soon as we entered the house. She fried breadfruit, and served it with boiled fish and taro. A pot of brak (much like taro but coarser) was boiling all the while. She cooked sitting down, the bamboo flooring of the kitchen being on the same level with the open fireplace. She tended the fire under the big iron pot of brak with bent bamboo tongs. She cooked our meal in a smaller pot set on a little Japanese stove, feeding the flame with coconut leaves. She served Dois and me with one fish each on a platter, an open dish of breadfruit, and a covered dish of taro. She placed between us an empty plate for fish bones and a small teapot of water on a small tray with two very dirty glasses which she rinsed and wiped with her hands. She gave me a fork and a spoon. Dois took his spoon from his handbag, wiped it on his shirttail, and we began to eat. She remained in the kitchen which was partially hidden from us by a low partition. After the meal Dois called her to bring a bowl of water for me to wash my fingers and his spoon. He returned that universal utensil to his handbag and took out a worn toothpick made of coconut leaf midrib. Two cats ate with us, but Mrs. Dois did not. We ate all of our fish except the heads. These and the remains of the taro and breadfruit Mrs. Dois took to the kitchen and ate. We continued to sit and smoke and talk for another hour.

It might be supposed that such domestic matters as sex-grouped dining are nothing more than a common-sense recognition that men prefer the company and talk of men and that women are just as happy that they do. That the Palauans view it as an expression of status seems evident, however, for the separation is geared into a separation of men on public occasions. Titled men eat together, the others eat with women and children when there is an inter-village feast and the number of headmen is large. When there are only a few of them, they are joined by retired chiefs and as many other elderly men as can be accommodated by separate servings on large food trays. There is thus a sliding scale of rank which is adjusted to circumstances; but always the young men eat from trays which they share with women and children. Individual servings as well as graded association are thus used to denote status.

Even when there are no guests, a woman will often serve her husband and her children and then eat what is left. This is partly a matter of convenience, but it fits comfortably into a well-established habit of following, of being second, whether it is in walking along a trail, greeting people, or bathing. It is so natural that women do not question its propriety—until well-wishers from other lands raise doubts in their minds. Men do not seriously consider tampering with this man-woman relationship, although one will occasionally make a gesture of enlightenment to impress American visitors, as Dois did at the marriage of his niece.

Dois decided that there was to be a "new-style" wedding, one of which the Americans to be invited would approve. Essentially this meant that the bride would be present at the nuptial feast. Consequently, after she had helped her female relatives prepare the food, Dois called her and asked her to put on her best dress and join the other guests, all of whom were men. He directed her to sit beside her father and share the food on his tray. He beamed at the Americans as he gestured for them to begin to eat. As is the custom, the rest of the company heartily and mutely attacked their food— except the bride and her father. They stared forlornly at their food, victims of acute indigestion and Americanization. Then she and the other women took the remains of the repast outside and ate under the trees across the yard.

A few women who have been converted to Christianity secretly resent their treatment. They talk about it among themselves and to sympathetic out- siders whom they trust. They recall that Herr Lange, an early missionary to the islands, pointed out that women do most of the work—making clothes, clearing trails, cooking, and gardening—while men talk and fish. Most of the time husbands are off somewhere, and when they come home they complain about their food, scold their wives for being lazy, and strike them if there is an argument.

So far these complaints are spasmodic and ineffectual. Most women do not feel imposed upon; they are as convinced of the rightness of Palauan custom as are the men. Not having known another way of life, they cannot view theirs objectively; they unquestioningly believe it to be good.

Here, for example, are Kai and Emei, a man and wife each about 35 years old. They have become interested in American customs and in their own as a result of many friendly questions and counter-questions over a period of months. They are trying to understand themselves and they like to talk about it. Both went to a village school under the Japanese, and Kai spent another year in Koror studying agriculture. He is a very large man for a Palauan. He is industrious and ambitious, proud of his strength, his knowl- edge and his skill, all of which are above average and all of which present him with a dilemma. He is torn between the urge to exercise his all-around ability and his determination to keep Emei in her Palauan woman's place. His pride and ambition impel him to overstep his masculine role, especially if he is aware that he is being observed by an American. He helps Emei break up clods and plant taro in their yard. He is apologetic about these activities, but explains that he has studied planting and is stronger in his arms. Emei is stronger at carrying things on her head. She says it all comes out about the same; men and women are equal in Palau, very different from the Japanese. A Japanese wife takes great pains to serve her husband. When he comes home she takes his shoes, wipes his face, and helps him into his house clothes. His food is served quickly and quietly. The Japanese wife addresses her husband in a "soft" language, timid and solicitous; he speaks to her in a sharp, firm tone.

Emei says she knows most about taro and that her gardens are her domain where she does as she likes. Kai agrees that this is so; she is an expert, much better than other women; but he is the one who decides which patches she should plant, which ones they will let others use, and who will inherit them, for they belong to his family. In any case, this doesn't matter, for they have plenty of land and can borrow more. Just last week they cleared a new patch because they are thinking of selling some taro in Koror. Emei is ready for more work now because their youngest child is three years old and she can spend more time gardening. She is not like other women, most of whom claim to be sick or use their children as an excuse for not working. Most of them lie around the house for ten days after the birth of a child. Emei has had five children, and each time she has been on her feet and working around the house in a few days. Emei adds that this is because she always goes through a ritual sweating process just after the birth of a child. It is an old custom and it is a good one. She doesn't know why it works, and it seems silly, but it restores a woman's strength quickly and it makes it possible to work in the sun all day without getting faint. It even helps her crippled hip. "Women are strong, men are weak," says Kai with pride.

4

Making a Living

ARO AND FISH are to the Palauan what bread and meat are to the ordinary American. They are regular fare, and no meal is considered to be complete unless both are included in it. They do not excite the appetite in the way rarer foods do, but they are nourishing and their supply is constant the year round. Luck, special care, or change of season provide such delicacies and festive foods as turtle, pigeon, pork, chicken, crab, lobsters, and clams in addition to or in place of fish. Extra effort and culinary pride may add rice, sweet potatoes, onions, manioc (cassava), breadfruit, and arrowroot to the daily supply of taro. In any case, a meal, in the thinking of a Palauan, draws upon both land and sea, one principally the domain of women, the other of men. Taro and fish are symbols of this ancient and fundamental balance of the sexes and of nature.

Farming is primarily a woman's occupation. Men clear new land of heavy growth and cut back borders of the forest that perpetually creep into old clearings. In a tropical land such as Palau, the battle against wild vegetation requires constant and laborious effort, even today when men use axes and heavy bush knives. In the past, before metal was introduced to the islands by traders, the men had only adzes and chisels with blades made of the thick, dense shell of the giant tridacna clam. Women assist in land clearing, attacking weeds and grass with knives, and from that point on the job is almost solely theirs.

There are four kinds of fields which take advantage of different types of land surface and permit variation in the food supply. The most desirable plots are in flat, low-lying areas that can be irrigated by water from a constant source. Small streams draining mountain slopes are tapped somewhere above the point where they enter the sea and their water is diverted into ditches which branch out to spread the stream into trickles around the borders of taro patches. These "wet" taro gardens are perennial producers and are tilled year after year. They must be fertilized to make them continuously pro-

25

ductive, and women do this by lifting out armloads of sticky mud, tossing grass and humus into the hole that is left, and then replacing the mud. Planting goes on throughout the year, and women so arrange it that there is always taro in one plot ready to eat at all times. The only implement they use is a sharp-pointed, narrow-bladed paddle.

Natural swamplands at the mouths of streams constitute the second kind of farming area. Some wet taro is grown there, but the principal crop is brak, which is like taro but larger and coarser. Plantings are made in the rich mud of one plot for three years, then shifted to another sector while the first lies fallow.

Clearings in the forested area near villages are used to cultivate a variety of taro which is called "dry" because it is watered only by rainfall and the moisture of the soil. Dry taro lives on the natural salts and minerals that accumulate on old forest floors. When crops have been planted in one spot for three years the soil begins to lose its capacity to support them. At this point a new clearing must be made in the forest and the old one allowed to lie idle for at least ten to fifteen years. Large trees are not chopped down; their bark is cut so that they will die and cease to shade the area. Smaller trees are hacked off. Their stumps are left standing but are charred by the burning of brush and leaves which completes the clearing operation. Dry taro is planted irregularly, wherever there is a free spot. The planting and harvesting implement is a digging stick. This is simply a sharpened stake which is thrust into the ground and wriggled about to loosen the soil.

The fourth type of cultivation is upland dry farming. Unlike the other three, it does not seem to be native to the islands. The hard soil must be broken with a three-pronged metal pick or hoe of Japanese manufacture and then shaped into mounds or ridges of loose earth into which grass and leaves are worked for enrichment. The small amount of surface water which runs down a hill slope may be channeled to the tilled area, but the principal source of water is by direct rainfall. It is in the preparation of these fields that men take their most active interest in agriculture, presumably because this type of farming has been introduced to the islands by European and Japanese men, rather than women, and the Palauans have accepted the association as natural. They do not obligate themselves to it, however, for women do most of the work except for the preparation of the ground. The crops they plant and tend are all foreign. Manioc and sweet potatoes are the most important; pineapples and a few vegetables, such as onions, are also grown to suit individual tastes.

The remaining food plants require little care, that little being the responsibility of men. The most important is the coconut, which propagates itself and provides a tangy, thirst-quenching liquid in the young nut, and a "milk" and an oil in the flesh of the fully ripened one. The milk is made by shredding the meat and mixing it with water. It is a universal sauce and a thickener for boiled foods. Coconut oil is used as a cosmetic as well as in cooking. The sap of the tree yields one luxury product, a sweet drink obtained by nipping and bleeding coconut buds. Inedible parts of the palm are equally important for other purposes. Trunks are used as logs in rough construction; leaves are woven into baskets and roof thatching; nut husks and shells make the hottest fire; and the fiber of the husk, called sinnet, is treated and woven into strings and ropes for all kinds of lashings that still hold more things together in Palau than do bolts, nails, or wire.

Papayas, arrowroot, bananas, sugar cane, and breadfruit reproduce by natural methods, although men do transplant the sprouts of the last three. One wild variety of banana bears a finger-sized inedible fruit and a very fibrous trunk from which a tough lashing is made. The Japanese manufactured rope from it, the so-called Manila hemp.

A remarkable characteristic of Palauan food crops is that they consist mostly of roots, not seeds, and of fleshy fruits, not hardy kernels that can be preserved. Along with these characteristics goes a year-around supply of the essential crops, which makes it unnecessary to lay up harvests during a dormant and unproductive season. Storage is therefore unnecessary, and it is not a feature of Palauan economy. There are no lean seasons for taro, bananas, and coconut. They bear perennially and are pulled fresh from the grove or garden. Famine, unless caused by a severe drought or typhoon, is unknown.

Men as farmers are exclusively identified with the growing of two non-food plants—pepper vines and tobacco. The pepper vine is planted at the base of coconut trees in the yard—where it can be guarded—and is trained to climb the trunks of the trees. Its leaves are highly valued because they are an indispensable ingredient in a chew of betel nut. The latter grows on tall slender palms that are also carefully watched. One-half a nut, which is about the size of a pecan, is powdered with lime and wrapped with a pepper leaf to make a chew that puckers the mouth and turns the saliva a reddish orange. The lime that goes into the mixture is made by heating fresh coral until it decomposes into a powder. It hastens the "kick" the chewer gets from the alkaloid in the nut. Betel chewing, and the incessant spitting that it provokes, is a universal habit among all adult Palauans, much to the dismay of American health authorities. Even the toothless may continue to enjoy this pleasure. When they can no longer chew, they pound their betel in small mortars which they carry with them.

Some men derive a small income from the sale of lime. A few have a surplus of betel to sell, but not many, for there never seems to be enough to meet the demands. It is comparable to tobacco in its physiological effects and in its appeal. Many Palauans find it too bland for their jaded taste, so they add a pinch of tobacco to their chew. This may be pure tobacco leaf or half a cigarette, paper and all.

The tobacco grown in Palau undoubtedly was introduced by the Europeans long ago. Despite the demand for it, only a few men know how to cultivate and treat it successfully today. It is easier to buy imported plugs, twists, and cigarettes—if one has the money—than to raise the local variety. Because of the demand, American cigarettes have become the leading import of the islands. Unlike betel chewing, smoking is a man's vice. A few young women furtively puff a cigarette when they can get one, but men frown on this brashness, as do the older women.

Palauan women are said to be afraid of the sea, and they probably are, for the men make it plain that it is not the place for women to frequent. Little girls are taught that they enter it at their peril. They are not expected to understand its mysteries. They may sail over it with men and collect sea urchins in it, and they may punt rafts around the lagoon close to shore and play around its edges; but otherwise they leave it to their fathers and brothers.

The most common type of fishing and the most uniformly productive one makes use of a long-shafted spear with thin metal barbs. This is the device for capturing the myriad forms of small fish which inhabit the lagoon, none of them more than ten inches long, many not over half that. They dart through the shallow water from one tiny pool to another or from one coral crag to another, seeking food or fleeing when they are disturbed. It takes a practiced eye to see more than a streak as they flash in all directions, and an even more amazing reaction speed to pin one to the sandy bottom with a spear. Seeking them at low tide on the reef a fisherman probes the crannies and the undercut bases of coral heaps, jabbing blindly in the dark recesses, rolling and threshing to keep his balance as the waves wash over him. Inside the reef where the water is quiet, he slowly and quietly stalks a likely pool then jabs at the nearest prey that attempts an escape. Or, most exciting of all, he sets off in hot pursuit of one on which he has fixed his eye and runs it to its death.

Old men, too slow of eye and limb to wield a spear, resort to nets. Of these there are several kinds, but the favorite requires a technique that kindles the old spirit of the chase if not its vigorous action. Two nets are required, one for each hand. They are shaped like the wing of a bird and are small and light enough to carry at the sides, flat side down. The fisherman cautiously approaches a knee-deep pool, his nets at the ready. When he reaches a bunch of seaweed he thrusts the nets down on both sides of it, kicking it if nothing happens. If he stirs up a nest, he plunges his nets down again and again hoping to intercept some of the fish in their frantic dashes.

Spear and net fishing are for the fair-weather months. So is the collection of clams and sea urchins by women and children. On dark nights, when there is not a breath of air and the lagoon is utterly placid, crab and clam fishing is best, too. This is the time for torches of coconut leaves or lanterns, for their light fascinates and immobilizes patches of sea life within its reach. It is a ghostly sight to see a quiet, black lagoon laced with distant, slowly weaving dots of light. A good fisherman, working until dawn, can collect as many as twenty crabs on such a night.

With the arrival of the tradewinds, beginning in January, the still-water activities are interrupted and there follows a slack season which everybody complains about. For days at a time during this three-month period many meals must be served without fish, only the most energetic men being able to catch enough for their families. The wind roils the sand on the lagoon floor and riffles the surface of the water, making such a complex refraction pattern that it is difficult to aim accurately. This is the season for traps. They are lattice-worked cages with tricky openings that invite entry but baffle the unobservant fish as they try to escape from them. They are placed with their openings landward, on coral heads some distance offshore but well within the reef.

Drugging fish is boy's play rather than man's work. It is engaged in by men, nonetheless, when they have nothing more important or amusing to do. Usually two or three cooperate in collecting the leaves of a narcotic plant, mashing them in sand, and casting the mixture over pools of still water. The lifeless fish soon begin to float to the surface and can be landed with a flick of a paddle.

Fish drives require the cooperation of many men. They are organized as a part of some community enterprise at which many guests are expected and must be fed. The drive itself is exciting, and men of all ages participate. A holiday atmosphere prevails and there is a great deal of shouting and wasted but happily expended energy. The preparation for this frolic is, however, hard work. Coconut fronds are woven into two long lines so that they form a curtain when the lines are stretched in an arc across the lagoon. As the arc is drawn into a circle, a large pocket is formed from which only the more desperate or courageous fish can escape by dashing through the leaf barrier. The rest are netted and speared in a wild melee as the encircling lines are gathered in and the pocket becomes smaller and smaller.

The flesh and shell of the turtle have always been highly valued in Palau. The flesh is a feast delicacy, so rare in the past that it was reserved for the grand entertainments of wealthy men. The custom was so well established that no common person would dare serve turtle without his chief's permission. If he were fortunate enough to capture one, he presented it to a chief who rewarded him either with some of its flesh or in some other acceptable way.

Another delicacy, not especially reserved for the wealthy, but usually served by them, is the flesh of the wild pigeon. This bird is very small, hardly enough for a man's meal, and it is an exasperating target for a clumsy hunter. The Palauans still hunt them with a bow and arrow, but more often with a blowgun. Both weapons are silent in action, an important consideration, for the hunter can conceal himself under trees where the pigeons rest and pick them off one by one without the remainder of the flock being alarmed. This is especially true of the blowgun, for it is simply a cane tube, seven or eight feet long, through which a dart is projected with remarkable force by a sharp puff of breath.

Domesticated animals were unknown in Palau until their introduction by Europeans. Chickens and pigs are now raised for their flesh. They are, however, definitely feast goods. A chicken may be killed for a family dinner if there is a surplus. Pigs are never killed unless there are enough people to consume the flesh within a day or two, for it does not keep. Eggs are not eaten except by unsuspecting Americans who are known to like them and who get them in all stages of decomposition and maturation, served by solicitous hosts who search the bushes to locate nests when their distinguished guests with strange tastes arrive.

Anciently, women made their own garments and those of their husbands and children, as well as other articles, from native materials. They pounded the inner bark of a certain tree to make a crude tapa, a pliable, fibrous cloth which was used by the men for a breech cloth. For themselves they made a "grass" skirt—short, thick bundles of fibers, one hanging from a cord at the waist in the front, another and larger one in back. They made pottery vessels of many shapes and uses. They wove mats of coconut and pandanus leaves for floor and wall covering and baskets of the same material for carrying goods.

In handicraft, men made their most important contributions through their skill in woodworking. They were the builders of several kinds of canoes, including some outriggers that carried sails and as many as fifty passengers. The canoes were thin and deep on the beam so that they skimmed the water under a stiff wind. They were ornately carved and inset with designs in shell inlay. The same was true of the old-fashioned Palauan houses, which were masterpieces of architecture, considering the time and the place. They were made of heavy, weather- and termite-resistant timbers, and were the most substantial dwellings in the Pacific from Java to Easter Island. Their posts and frames were massive, their walls and roofs of woven reeds and thatch—just the right combination to survive the typhoons which strike periodically and spend their force on the leafy parts of the structures. Some of these dwellings, and the men's club houses, which were built like them, are still being used. They have, however, outlasted the custom of building them, for now they are being replaced by flimsy buildings of tin and planed boards, copied from Japanese and American models.

The Palauans can no longer live on the resources of their islands. Over the years of outside contact they have become acquainted with foreign foods and manufactured goods, and many of these importations they now regard as necessities. They want them and feel deprived when they cannot have them. Heading the list among foods is rice, for which they acquired a taste by Japanese example. The Japanese attempted to induce the islanders to become self-sufficient in this respect, concentrating their efforts on the men. The results were disappointing. They were not able to get beyond the schoolboys, and today no one grows rice.

There are other necessities that cannot or will not be produced: tools, cloth, household utensils, kerosene, sugar, American cigarettes—and *canned* fish. Since Palau is at the end of a long and wavering supply line, all of these items are scarce and costly. All districts have small stores, mostly with unstocked shelves and intermittent hours. Stocks and sales rise and fall with the irregular arrival of goods: all the most desirable items are sold out in a few hours or days, leaving a forlorn scattering of pale canned peas and oversize boots from one shipment to the next.

A necessity for foreign money has evolved along with the demand for imported goods. The greatest single source of income is government employment. The various departments of the American administration unit in Koror employ several hundred Palauans in various capacities. Most are unskilled laborers or semiskilled technicians such as boat tenders, heavy machine operators, and mechanics. A few work in the government offices as clerks, interpreters, messengers, or trainees; or in the school system; or on the police force; or in the hospital. Their pay ranges from approximately $300 annually to a maximum of $2,000.

Another source of foreign money is through the export of trochus shells, which brings several thousand dollars to the islands each year. Men must dive deeply on the ocean side of the reef to collect this mollusc, the shells of which are exported to Japan where they are cut into buttons. The sale of copra brings the largest share of the total cash income from the island resources. It requires no capital outlay and little labor. To produce it, a man husks the coconut over a sharpened stake fixed in the ground, cracks the shell in half, and dries the meat in the sun or over a slow fire. The meat must be pried out of the shell and cut in smaller pieces to be properly aged before shipping. Three hundred nuts will bring a man from four to six dollars.

Individual enterprise is hampered by the network of economic obligations and services in which every Palauan is enmeshed. Men who attempt to set themselves up in shopkeeping, barbering, or in any other private undertaking find that they have plenty of business but little income. They do not feel that they can charge their relatives for services or goods; and their relatives either assume that they should not be required to pay or are inclined to charge what they get against obligations owed them on other accounts by the struggling businessman. Consequently a man's stock and time dwindle away with no cash returns to put back in the business. In addition to this discouragement, there is the old Palauan custom which makes it undesirable for a man to appear prosperous. All men, by their own protests, are poor. To be otherwise is to invite all kinds of maneuvers to wheedle and coerce a man out of his money.

5

Serving the Community

COMMUNITY SERVICE has always been recognized as a primary obligation of Palauan men and women of all ages. Whenever anything needs to be done that is in the interest of all village or district residents, the chiefs issue an order to one or more of the appropriate work units. These groups are vestiges of the old men's and women's clubs, their labor function having outlived many others that were replaceable or less essential. At one time they contributed much more than physical labor to the welfare and vigor of village life.

Club life flourished and was elaborately organized until fifty years ago. Men and women had their sets of clubs, the sets separated according to age but also divided into two major groups or moieties. Each male unit occupied a club house. Women's groups did not, although they were permitted to use those of the men for special purposes. Each male club was led by a man of the highest ranking family in the community. He represented the membership in its relations with all nonmembers and was responsible to the community for the behavior of his fellows. Fines were paid to him by members for their infractions of club rules. In addition, he imposed penalties on outsiders for violation of his club's prerogatives and was responsible for payments for offenses committed by his associates. Each club also had leaders in war and other activities. Ideally these men were all members of the most important lineages, or were at least entitled to respect on the basis of family connections. Without such prestige to generate support, no club could function.

Men spent most of their free time in the club houses. They slept there and kept their personal articles there. They usually ate at home, but on occasions their meals were brought to them at the club. Club-house areas were avoided not only by women but by members of other clubs, especially when a meeting was being held or some activity was under way. Internal affairs were kept secret, and anyone who pried was punished. Unless a person had been invited, it was advisable for him to stay away from the club house.

Warfare, or talk about it, occupied much of the time of the young men. Their clubs functioned independently of each other in attack and defense; they competed in the taking of heads and in other war honors. All were under orders of the chiefs but once given a command they were allowed the freedom to execute it to their benefit as well as that of their community. Fighting was mainly for the purpose of forcing a payment of money for a crime, or as an indemnity, or for favors rendered. Personal revenge was on incentive, as was the desire for a reputation as a fighter; but money always entered into the schemes and demands for satisfaction. The chiefs of one district sometimes secretly conspired with those of another for an assault on a third, the first district attacking while the second offered refuge to the women and children of the attacked group. After the siege the conspirators divided the money collected for the protection given to the women. The chiefs, not the fighting men, were paid, for regardless of personal satisfaction, warfare was a patriotic service and its monetary rewards were for the purpose of increasing district prestige.

The labor force represented by clubs was also controlled by village or district chiefs. A club or a combination of more than one could be called upon to build or repair a street or a public building. Any able-bodied man or woman could in fact be conscripted for labor or for attendance on a chief in the furtherance of community welfare. In addition, the young men's clubs operated as a police force. When a regulation was announced by the chiefs, one or more of the clubs was designated to enforce it. Its members were empowered to act even though an infraction of the rules called for the punishment of a high-ranking person, the chiefs themselves not being immune. The club was granted the privilege of fining an offender and keeping the money for itself.

Young women's clubs were a special asset to their communities. Under orders of their chiefs, their members were sent to another village to live in the club house of men of approximately their own age. There they waited on their male companions, sometimes attaching themselves to a man of their choice, sometimes catering impartially to several. They stayed several days or months, depending on the agreement reached previously by the chiefs of the two districts or villages involved. Some of the attachments led to honorable marriage, for no stigma attached to premarital relationships under these circumstances. In fact, girls were praised for their ability to please their companions, such pleasures being registered by a payment of money. The money was given in their individual names—if they merited such recognition in the opinion of their consorts—to their guardian, who was a father, a brother, or a mother's brother. But in addition, the chief of the men's district paid a really valuable piece of money to the chief of the girls' district. This was an important consideration, indeed the primary one, for this and victory in warfare were the principal means of enriching district treasuries. Many an inconspicuous village has risen to prominence through payments for its girls, and pieces of money are cherished in memory of the girls' patriotism.

Women themselves were not in a position to object to this exercise of statecraft. Some might be exempted, especially if they were members of important families and it was considered inadvisable to tempt them into love matches which would interfere with marriage plans for them. Married as well as unmarried women were conscripted, either with or without their husband's consent. In fact, if a husband was lazy, or delinquent in payments to his wife's people, this device offered a means to compensate for the liability that he represented. As a last resort, women were kidnapped by their club members if either they or their husbands refused to cooperate peaceably.

In all their activities the clubs in one moiety cooperated and assisted each other in competition with their counterparts in the opposite moiety. Each club tried to excel its rival in speed, amount of labor, contributions, war honors, or police action. Ordinarily, rivals would not be given the same assignment because their competitiveness was likely to develop into open conflict. In all instances, rivalries were supposed to be good natured, and they were accompanied by joking and a display of friendliness. They were nonetheless serious matters to which much thought and effort were given; and they offered a fertile field for the Palauan penchant for behind-the-scenes scheming and intrigue.

The elaborate development of club life began to disintegrate many years ago. It lost much of its vigor under the German regime, and the Japanese helped to perpetuate only those aspects of it that were congenial to their purposes. The Americans have given no official recognition to what remains of club life, but the Palauans find that remnant necessary to maintain themselves as a functioning society. Club houses have decayed or have been destroyed; the sexual division of the population is still clear-cut, but age grouping within the divisions has become less precise; the partitioning into moieties and most of the activities associated with that separation no longer exist.

The Japanese paid most attention to the age group they called the *seinen dan*. Membership in it was based on completion of the education offered the Palauans. Both boys and girls belonged, but each sex had its own organization. Individuals were admitted to the group by a formal application which was acted upon by the district school teacher, the real leader of both the undergraduate and graduate groups. These associations of school children and of graduates were primarily work groups serving the community. They were indoctrinated with Japanese ideology and to some extent the program of their training followed the familiar pattern of youth organizations in Japan and in other parts of the world. Health, physical exercise, and "culture" were stressed. The older men, called *ngarasubuyas,* were also expected to perform certain duties. Chiefs were responsible for the behavior of their people and conveyed the regulations of the authorities to them. They functioned as they had in the past, but without freedom in their capacities as rulers and judges.

This situation continues at the present time except that, because of a lack of direction on the part of American authorities, and because of an uncertainty on the part of the Palauans as to what is expected of them, the outlines of the *seinen dan* as a distinct group have become blurred and indefinite. It is still essentially a community labor organization, as are the other age groups.

Their leaders receive orders from the chiefs for all corporate tasks, and in general they take their assignments seriously. The full membership does not always turn out for a given project, and consequently the labor force is sometimes quite small. No fines or other punishments are laid upon those who fail to appear, but people who persist in absenting themselves are rebuked by the chiefs, as are those who are absent on a given occasion when some important job is to be done. The female *seinan dan* are regularly called upon to weed the trails and clean up the areas around public buildings and cemeteries. Sometimes the older women, whose organization parallels the *ngarasubuyas,* are also called upon for one of these tasks. The *seinan dan* men are conscripted to make all of the village improvements, such as the building of stores and meeting houses and the clearing of areas for new buildings.

There is almost always something for some group to do. At times there is a surge of activity that takes up most of the time of the able-bodied men. The work load on them has been especially burdensome since World War II, for the Palauans have had to repair damages and rehabilitate their villages themselves. In addition, several districts are now being prodded into modernization projects by progressive leaders who aim at approximations to American living standards.

Many of the young men now fret under their load of community obligations. They have the example of American individualism before them and they are driven by personal needs under a cash economy to work in their own interests. Many grumble among themselves that they can buy no store goods even when they are available, for they have had no time to work for themselves. Some confide that they would like to abandon the community-service system altogether and substitute for it, if necessary, some form of taxation to pay for the work that must be done.

The system still functions best under the drive of pride and the excitement of competition. District rivalry has smoldered over the years of foreign domination, with occasional flare-ups over political or prestige issues. Under the Americans, a new development appears to be shaping up which challenges the traditional ranking of the districts. Ngarard and Pelelieu have always occupied an inferior position in district ratings, but now their chiefs claim that they are the most "progressive" in the islands, using this new measure of supremacy to challenge the leadership of Koror and Melekiok. They conspire to assist each other and are aided in their designs by their strategic relationships with the Americans. The scheming for advantage by the contenders in this struggle necessarily affects everyone within their jurisdictions. Men have had to spend considerable time away from their own work to substantiate the claim of their districts to be "first."

The Koror Community Center is a monument to Palauan capacity to produce cooperatively under the stimulus of competition. The Center consists essentially of a club house constructed of native materials and in native style but very much larger than its prototype, the men's club house. It was built almost entirely by the Palauans and is for their exclusive use. From the Americans they received only the most necessary material assistance, but much stimulation, advice, and encouragement. In fact, the Center was an American idea which had to be sold to the Palauans in such a way that they could accept it as their own. Its purpose was manifold, but, briefly, it was to inspire a feeling of Palauan unity and pride that ignored the limits of district, village, and family loyalties.

Few Palauans grasped this lofty design, but many of them wanted a building of their own in the town of Koror, the hub of economic and political action; and the rest could not afford to let themselves be excluded. When several contenders for American patronage leaped at the chance to support the project, their adversaries did likewise. Planning committees were formed and their meetings well attended out of fear of losing influence or a chance to propose something. Craftsmen who carved and painted the thematic panels on the gables of the club house vied for public praise of their skill and at the same time selected episodes and heroic acts for portrayal that proclaimed the glory of their clans and districts. Even ordinary people, old and young, claimed the right to contribute some special material or service and receive credit for it. Some villages took pride in supplying a specialty, such as a kind of timber or a thatching material, for which their localities are famous. Old men, reviving their ability, braided the coconut fiber used throughout the building to hold its parts together and made thousands of fathoms of cordage and rope. They also made many of the hundreds of strips of thatch necessary to cover the immense roof of the building. Women and children were kept busy with the specialties reserved for them—feeding the men and cleaning up.

The result of this inspired activity was that a huge building and an adjacent recreational area was rushed to completion in a little over two months, to the astonishment of Palauans and Americans alike. Once the idea of contest was implanted, the enthusiasm for the project was self-generating. The Palauans are jealous of their alleged pre-eminence among the Micronesians and they were flattered by the High Commissioner's decision to make the club house a pilot project, and by this evidence of the government's attention to their needs. They were stimulated to greater efforts by the sincere expressions of admiration, surprise, and encouragement by the local American community. Crews of workmen donated over 3,000 man days to it. An impressive quantity of free food flowed from the outer districts to Koror where it was prepared and served by volunteer crews of women. Individuals as well as groups contributed cash to buy extra frills, although the plan stipulated that no one was to be called on for cash. Palauan enthusiasm was contagious, and many Americans responded by freely contributing their time and skills as needed.

The Center has not accomplished an overnight miracle of consolidating the Palauans or of making them happy with their lot. More than a club house is needed to change such time-honored and deep-seated motivations as the Palauan compulsions to succeed and excel. It was, after all, these drives that built the Center.

6

Making Money

BEING PALAUAN is being interested in money, in the same sense that being American is being interested in money. It is not the whole of existence, but it strikes the outsider as commanding or coloring a great part of it. There are Palauans, as there are Americans, who deliberately reject a materialistic definition of success and the competition that goes with it. There are others who disclaim the ambition to be measured in these terms while at the same time they are motivated by it. But whether they like it or not, none can deny or escape the impress that the striving for wealth gives to his life.

This is not a recent development, for Palauans had several forms of money when they were visited by Captain Wilson in 1783. All are quite different from the coin and currency of modern nations. They do not have the seal of government on them and the supply of the most important kind, so-called "men's money," can never be increased because its source is unknown. All of it came to the islands centuries ago, presumably through trade with people to the west. When the traffic that brought it ceased, mystery and legend began to replace whatever facts might have been known about its origins.

Men's money is composed of three materials: a hard, glassy pottery, a variegated porcelain, and old imperfect glass. There are a large number of types within each of these categories: bars, discs, spheres, and tubes. They range in size from 1/4 to 3 inches. Most of them are perforated for stringing. All except the glass pieces are still in use, so much so that social position and political power depend on the possession of a certain number of them. American money is now acceptable in part as a substitute, but by no means wholly so. Crucial events, such as births, marriages, and deaths, must still be socially validated by a transfer of native money from the male to the female side of the family.

The names of the shapes and sizes of these many bits of pottery and glass, and the values attached to them, make little sense to an outsider and only slightly more to the average Palauan. The mystery is not entirely due to the confusion of accident or practical necessity. It is in part a deliberate complication, for knowledge of the different classes and grades of money is a cultivated art. It is, moreover, a jealously guarded prerogative of chiefs and specialists; few ordinary people even know the names of the various denominations. The system is not uncontrolled, but it operates to the advantage of the few who are in a position to manipulate it. For them, the circulation of money is an exciting game wherein salesmanship, social dominance, and deception are assets.

Women have their own kind of money. It is subsidiary to and less valuable than men's. It is made of turtle shell, cut and molded to form small trays not more than 10 inches in length. The material for them is near at hand, though not easy to get. Theoretically the supply is unlimited, and trays continue to be made now as in the past. The increase resulting from more efficient means of capturing turtles has not seriously inflated the value of the trays, for the older ones are rated above recent products much for the same reason that individual pieces of men's money have acquired distinction.

Turtle-shell trays and fragments of foreign pottery and glass have never been indispensable to life in Palau. Plenty of food, good shelter, and a rich variety of useful goods have always been available to anyone who has wanted to produce them himself. Nevertheless, both men's and women's money have been geared into the subsistence economy in such a way as to stimulate it to an output beyond the essentials of a livelihood, and even beyond a modest luxury and surplus production level. The stimulation is in the interest of gaining prestige, and very often it operates to produce a wasteful excess of labor and goods. In addition, money has been injected into social, political, and religious affairs to such an extent that the Palauan outlook on life has a distinctive materialistic bent. Everything owned by others must be paid for; and many things are paid for in Palau that people in other parts of the world take or use as a natural right. As a result, the whole superstructure of purpose, attitude, and social interaction would collapse if by some selective catastrophe all Palauan money were suddenly to disappear.

Since money has this importance, it is essential that every person have a certain amount of it to his credit, even though he may never see it or know just how much of the family reserve is his. There are several ways that a credit can be built up today, and still others that have been outlawed or discarded under German and Japanese rule.

One of the approved ways of making money, of course, is to earn it. In aboriginal times the exercise of talent had a greater scope than it now has. It also commanded a better price. There were, for example, professional canoe makers, tatooers, song composers, carvers, healers, and priests as well as house builders such as there are today. They profited from their abilities in two ways: by selling their services and by accepting apprentices who paid them for instruction. Their earning power was greater than that of the few remaining specialists for another reason: they enjoyed a virtual monopoly of their craft. There were, presumably, a certain number of amateurs, because not everyone could afford to pay for everything he wanted. They must have been few, however, because every person had the help of his relatives and they collectively could provide the prestige necessities. In any event, no one with pretensions to rank would think of making his own canoe or building his own house. This is still true with respect to house building.

All service for pay operates on the cardinal rule that, for corporate benefit, it must be performed for someone outside the lineage. No one collects money from a maternal kinsman. The rule holds and is most evident in the case of routine, unprofessional services and physical labor. At this point it gears into a complex system of work and compensation that is channeled through the domestic unit of man, wife, and child. To put it starkly—as few Palauans put it to themselves—the ordinary domestic duties of a woman and her children are conceived as work done for her husband and their father. He or his heir pays for this service, when either he or they die, with pieces of money given to their closest male relative, who retains and uses the money in their names. The husband and father is therefore a key outsider for the maternal kinsmen. He is a more constant and certain source of income to a group of such kinsmen than are others who have only an occasional or single professional service to offer.

This system of pay for domestic service, which is called *omulu'ul*, requires that food and labor be exchanged for money and, at times, land. The exchange is regularized by the further requirement that a wife, her children, and others in her lineage always tender food and labor to her husband and he always compensates them with money or land, never the reverse. A money debt is not paid with money nor a food or work debt in kind. There are other kinds of exchanges outside this system, as when a personal service is paid with service, and when borrowed food is returned. These reciprocations are between relatives, occasionally between very good friends and neighbors. They never involve Palauan money.

The *omulu'ul* system is best explained by stating the three principles on which it operates. The first is that only the oldest male in a group of maternal lineage mates can actually hold and control his own money and land. He also controls the money and land of his siblings and that of his sister's children. Younger brothers do not administer the wealth that they have inherited and that is considered to be theirs. As young men, they neither hold nor control the money that they earn from their own efforts. As they grow older they may, with the consent of their lineage head, gradually assume more control.

The second principle is that individuals owe their services and the products of their labor to their lineage head in return for his guidance, protection, and financial support. They are obliged to supply him with food derived from their fishing activities or, in the case of women, from their work in the taro fields and other agricultural activities. Not only do they supply food for his household needs; they are also obliged to work for their lineage head when he is called upon to serve others as a result of demands upon him through the system of exchanging money for services. These are obligations that they inherit by reason of their birth in his matrilineal group. In return for their services, the lineage head is obliged to support them and maintain their social position. He is therefore responsible for making arrangements and payments at the times of their births, marriages, and deaths. In short, the mother's Lrother is the financial agent and administrator for his immediate matrilineal kinship group.

The third principle, and one likely to lead to misunderstanding of the system unless it is grasped, is that the fundamental prerogative of a lineage head to act as agent for his dependents can be transferred. This must be done by a well-understood agreement. By such an agreement a man renounces his right to administer the affairs of a given dependent, but he does not break off his kinship ties with him. There is not even a complete denial of financial interest in such a former dependent. The mother's brother, in effect, simply sells his dependent's services for a period of time, normally for the lifetime of the latter. In the end he must be compensated for this loan of his relative.

The relinquishment of control by the mother's brother is by no means uncommon. In fact, it is so routine as to be the rule rather than the exception, because the person who normally takes over the control of a dependent is his own father. It is not only regular procedure for a mother's brother to relinquish his prerogative in this respect; it is expected that the father will substitute for him.

The prerogative of a mother's brother to administer the fortunes of his dependents is normally relinquished in part also to husbands. When a woman gets married it is with the implicit assumption that she owes food and service to her husband. She is not freed of her obligation to help her mother's brother, but she is expected to divert most of her energies toward the service of her husband. In this she is encouraged and aided by her uncle and her brothers because they, through her, are entitled to a money return, and sometimes compensation in land. By the same token, a man also diverts a part of his energies from the service of his mother's brother to that of his sister's husband in return for money paid either directly to him or to his uncle.

In this game the wife has little or nothing to say. Her allegiance is naturally, as the Palauans see it, to her brothers and to her mother's brother—not to her husband. She is, in fact, in conspiracy with her blood relatives to get the most money possible out of her husband and his relatives. If she were to be lax in this respect she would be regarded as ungrateful to her relatives. The ideal type of woman is one who works hard in the interests of her brothers and sisters. Her labor is only indirectly for the benefit of her husband, since the primary objective is to get money for her kin group. It is for this reason that Palauan women are said to be the source of money.

Women carry on exchanges among themselves. Their activities in this respect parallel those of the men but the two systems do not overlap. Women always deal in only their kind of money—that is, in turtle-shell trays. A woman never gives or receives pieces of men's money. Their exchanges take place on the same occasions as those of the men, but they are subordinate to the men's activities. Just as a husband owes only money to his wife's brother in compensation for food and service, so his sister is required to pay his wife so many shell trays for her share of the same food and service. Similarly, just as a man is obliged to give money to the brother of his daughter-in-law, so a woman gives shell trays to her daughter-in-law. In all instances, money and trays are classed together, and both are set over against food and service.

Most men are financially dependent on their fathers or lineage heads all of their lives. There is one way, however, that an ambitious man can achieve some measure of independence. He can, with the consent of his father or uncle, hold an *o'oraul* for the purpose of receiving contributions of money from his friends and relatives. He also takes care to invite his sisters' husbands, for they are expected to contribute most liberally. The contributions of these men and those of friends are considered to be loans. Those of the host's own relatives were once regarded as gifts; now they too tend to be treated as loans. The host's wife and her relatives, as usual, are the suppliers of the feast that must precede the collection of money.

Men never release their money willingly or graciously but cling to it as if it were a part of them. This tenacity exists not only because money is dear but also because a generous man could not long survive the many pressures put upon him. Every transfer entails prolonged negotiations and various gambits and counter-strategies. The two parties to the negotiations do not confront each other face to face but use intermediaries. The intermediaries are chosen for their ability to use flattery, persuasive arguments, and clever interpretations to induce acceptance of the offers made by their group.

Bargaining takes place at any time there is a transfer of money, regardless of the nature of the occasion. The same reluctance to pay for a bride at marriage prevails at death, when the husband's relatives must join together in paying a respectable sum of money to the wife's male relatives. No payment is settled in advance. The price of a canoe or a house is what the workman can force or wheedle out of the buyer after the job is completed. The reluctance to part with money is also displayed when a man borrows money from his invited guests at an *o'oraul*. Each person, on all of these occasions, holds back what he must pay for a seemingly interminable time before he finally hands it over with great deliberation in movement.

When the floor of the club house in Adas had to be replaced it was rumored that Menglo, the father of the carpenter, was going to demand $800 for the job. This was an extravagant charge, for the work could have been done with a fair profit for $200. But the building is claimed by the titled men of the village, and chiefs always have to pay more than common men. Their solution to the problem of paying this amount was to request all of the middle-aged men of the district to consider themselves chiefs for the occasion. All were addressed by the honorific term *rupak* and they had no option but to submit to the flattery and the request. This meant that they had to raise money fast, and the way to do this is by holding an *o'oraul*. Everybody, including the chiefs, took this course. On one day five were held in the same village. Since many of the same men were involved each time, the tangle of debts and counter-debts almost produced a financial crisis.

When the day for settlement arrived, thirty-nine men of varying ranks were assembled in the club house by 10 o'clock in the morning. The first chief of the district sat in his accustomed place by the first door on the right. Honored guest chiefs from two other villages sat on each side of the front entrance. Other titled men occupied the places assigned by tradition to their rank on either side of a doorway. The "chiefs for a day" filled in wherever there was a space. Menglo was one of these, and he sat at the end of the building farthest away from the first chief, who was the strategist for the buyers of the floor and his principal adversary in the bargaining maneuvers to come. Because of the differences in their rank, the interplay could not be so straightforward as to directly involve these two men.

There is no rule against a man speaking for himself in opposition to a chief, but it is better not to. Low rank talking to high rank calls for reserve and acquiescence. Furthermore, a low-ranking man is a novice in the protocol of dealing with chiefs. He feels tongue tied and powerless. Like the lay citizen in court, he may lose his case by saying the right thing at the wrong time. He needs a skilled advocate. Following custom, Menglo had therefore brought with him a spokesman who held a title and by good fortune was also the maternal uncle of the carpenter, Menglo's son. As speaker for his side, the first chief designated a chief of approximately the same rank as Menglo's spokesman. All cross-communication, from one end of the house to the other, was between these two intermediaries, one of whom was higher in rank than the man he represented, the other lower.

Before they could begin the negotiations, the buyers (the "chiefs") had to assess their resources. Ordinarily this would have been done before the appearance of the other party; otherwise the procedure was the usual one. Middle-aged subordinate relatives crouched before their family representatives to offer them one or two dollars; young men and women handed their contributions in the doorways to be passed to their leaders. The first chief placidly but firmly directed the canvass, having at his command three attendants who quietly and deferentially shuttled between him and the other chiefs, carrying information and directions. Two men busy with paper and pencil sat at his side, setting down names and sums. Finally they arrived at the conclusion that $621 was all they could count on.

Menglo never spoke aloud. When the negotiations opened, the chief who represented him requested $800. This initiated an exchange of repartee between the two spokesmen, most of which was designed to draw laughter and relieve the tension. The chiefs had the advantage, not only because of rank and numbers, but also because each, as he thought of it, passed along an intimidating witticism to their spokesman who embellished it as he saw fit.

By one o'clock it was evident that Menglo was ready to accept the chiefs' offer, and their spokesman was sent to huddle with him in private. He returned to his place to announce that a price of $600 was agreed upon. The messengers then collected the individual contributions on platters and the tellers verified their count. After the money had been given to Menglo, the first chief directed his spokesman to make a laudatory speech commending

Menglo for his reasonable attitude and announcing that an extra $21 was being given to him by way of appreciation.

It was about 2:30 when the first chief directed that the food be served. Women brought it on trays to the doorways and attendants placed it before the men, following the chief's instructions. Several times there were mutterings about who should receive what, especially when it came to serving the untitled "chiefs." Quietly and decisively the first chief asserted that he was the "master of the way" and proceeded to direct the placement of the food trays and the sprigs of betel nut.

The men ate quickly and silently. The chiefs were given very large portions from which they took what they wanted and then handed their trays to their relatives outside. Everyone got something in proportion to his rank, down to Nial, a forlorn old widower who had been able to contribute only $.50. After the food had been cleared away, the lesser men unobtrusively drifted off. This was really not their party. The rest remained to talk until almost dark, as is the custom among important men.

7

Having a Family

THE SON OF Adelbai and the daughter of Kras had been living together for about two months when the two men decided they were ready to make the marriage settlement. On the appointed day the bride's sisters and her brothers and their wives met at her father's house early in the morning. They brought food with them which the women immediately began to cook over open fires in the yard and in the kitchen. The men sat on the floor around the walls of Kras' Japanese-style house, talking, smoking, and chewing betel until about noon when the food was ready.

In the meantime Adelbai and his helpers had gathered in his house to make up a purse for the marriage price. The groom was not present, for he had a job in Koror and could not get away. That did not matter because his finances were being managed jointly by his father and his mother's brother. Their partnership was due to the fact that his mother's brother had the Palauan money necessary to legitimize the union, while his father could contribute only American dollars. The bride price was their responsibility, but Adelbai intended to shift his part of it as much as possible to the men who owed him money. These men were principally his clan sisters' husbands; and that was why several of them and their wives were invited. Also present was a scattering of less certain sources of cash. Among them, and in keeping with the modern trend, were a few nonrelatives indebted to Adelbai and three or four clan brothers known to have American money. Ngiraoik, the second chief of the district, was also there. He sat apart from the rest, and from the bride's party when it arrived, to act as an impartial observer and advisor on procedure.

When it appeared that all of Adelbai's helpers had arrived, Ngiraoik directed an attendant to place a turtle-shell tray in front of him and named a man who could write to set down the contributions of each person. This was the new way, he said, and it wasn't quite proper. It was mixed up with the o'oraul, with people borrowing the bride price from friends and expecting their sons and younger brothers to help them. But Palauan customs were changing, everyone needed dollars, and so it was necessary to keep an account of the cash contributed. He and the older men would witness the Palauan money that changed hands. He went on to say that marriage was a serious business and that everyone should give all the money he could in order to make a good showing. Otherwise Kras and his relatives would be dissatisfied and the marriage might end in divorce. That, he warned, would call for an even more expensive settlement. He then indicated that the collection could begin.

There was no immediate response to his suggestion. A few men commented on his speech, and one or two asked questions. The rest gazed out the doorway or quietly talked among themselves of other things. There were a few jokes. Everyone seemed to be waiting for somone else to make the first move. At last the wealthiest of Adelbai's brothers-in-law beckoned for the attendant to bring the tray to him. He slowly unfolded a twenty-dollar bill and placed it on the tray. This gave the others an idea of what could be expected of them, and for the next hour they followed his lead, one by one, after long intervals and careful deliberation. No one else gave more than ten dollars. A younger brother of the groom gave $.85. Three of Adelbai's sisters gave a few dollars each, independently of their husband's contributions. Finally there was $100 on the tray and it was brought to Ngiraoik for his approval. It was then returned to Adelbai, who tucked it in his handbag. By that time the bride's party was beginning to arrive and with them the food.

After the meal was over everyone left the building except the two groups of men, one representing the bride, the other the groom. Adelbai drew out the $100 and put it on a tray. This was the point at which someone on the groom's side had to produce a piece of Palauan money. It was rather well understood that this person was to be his mother's brother, and, after a long private consultation with Adelbai, he carefully added a piece to the American currency. This was taken to Ngiraoik, who nodded his approval but directed that the Palauan money be covered by one of the bills. Kras took a quick look at the offer when it was brought to him and refused it. One hundred dollars was not enough and the Palauan money was not worthy of his daughter. Adelbai had to confer with his helpers again. Another fifty dollars was contributed, mostly by him. Another piece of Palauan money was substituted for the first and the tray was again sent to Kras. He was still not satisfied; the cash was acceptable but not the Palauan bead. This rebuff visibly upset its owner, but there was nothing he could do but substitute a more valuable piece. To everyone's relief, Kras accepted the third offer, and Adelbai praised his sound judgment in a little speech which he concluded with a gift of ten dollars, for "his good friend, Kras, personally."

As usual, with the tension relaxed, talk flowed freely and long. This time it turned to Ngiraoik's comments about changing marriage customs. It began with contrasts between the Japanese and the Palauan forms and went on to questions about the American style. Do Americans pay for their wives? Do they choose their own mates? Do they ever get divorced? This led Ngiraoik into a long description of the "real" Palauan way. It differed only in detail from present practices, but the differences loomed large in his perspective.

In former times, Ngiraoik said, important families kept a much closer watch on their children than they do now. All young people had love affairs that were carried on in secrecy, just as now; but parents were not blind and if they were members of a ranking family they put a stop to an undesirable affair at once.

Here Ngiraoik told a story which is known all over Palau and which is said to be true. It tells of a love affair between a young man of high rank and a girl from a low-class family. This was bad enough, but what made the match impossible was the fact that they were third cousins. In the beginning they did not know this, nor did their parents, for they belonged to different clans that came from different parts of the island. The great-grandfather of the boy was a brother of the great-grandmother of the girl, which made their children necessarily of different clans, since everyone belongs to the clan of his or her mother and must marry outside it. It just happened that in this case the love-struck pair were related to their sibling great-grandparents through males only, and over the generations this connection had been forgotten. This is the more understandable in that the boy's line had consistently married up the social scale while the girl's immediate forebearers had married down. When all this came to light the couple was forbidden to see each other again. They refused to submit and continued to meet secretly. Finally one night they loaded a canoe with food and other goods and set sail for the south, never to be heard of again.

This story can be expected to evoke expressions of sympathy for the lovers, especially if an American is present, and so it did on this occasion. The sympathy springs from the fact that marriage prohibitions are based not simply on blood ties but on the memory of them. Everyone knows that members of the same clan cannot be married; neither can the children of two brothers or of a brother and a sister even though they are of different clans. Everyone is further agreed that marriage between the children of these cousins and between their children is forbidden. Beyond that there is uncertainty and sometimes argument, the only universally agreed on rule being that marriage is permissible if a connection through the paternal lines of a couple has been forgotten. This usually means that their immediate ancestors have drifted apart geographically as well as genetically. Physical nearness also prevents the marriage of adoptive and natural children. If they or their descendants are separated, the memory of the foster sibling relationship is likely to fade away. Intermarriage of their descendants, like that of the descendants of true siblings, would be wrong. But, as Ngiraoik said with a laugh: "What can we do? All of us marry our sisters without knowing it." It was too bad that the couple in the story had to find out.

He added, and the rest of the men shook their heads sadly and agreed, that children were more respectful to their parents in the old days than they are now. They were also less forward in expressing their marriage intentions. If a match was acceptable, a couple only indirectly revealed their plans, usually by the boy spending more and more time around the girl's house, helping her father and eating there. He stayed later and later and finally began to spend the night there. If, after a couple of months, this arrangement was acceptable to all, plans were made to pay the bride price, just as Adelbai had done today.

An older man did not go through these preliminaries, Ngiraoik said, bcause a *rupak* is his own master. All that he did was to give a piece of money to the guardian of the woman he wanted to marry and then take her home with him. Of course, he had to pay for her later if he wanted to keep her. A young man could not do this; neither could he build a separate house as he sometimes does now. He and his wife had to live with her father until she became pregnant, at which time they moved into the house of her mother's brother. There they were royally treated, especially if their parents were wealthy. Her uncle hired a man to hunt and fish for them, and her kinswomen kept them supplied with large quantities of other good food. All of this had to be paid for later by the boy's guardian, who was usually his father. He also paid for a mid-wife, and for diviners, and for women who knew the magic to insure a successful delivery. If the forecasts were favorable, the girl was allowed to display a large piece of money on a cord at her throat which belonged to her lineage. At the sixth month of pregnancy there was another ceremony as important as the marriage itself. As at the time of marriage, food was supplied by the girl's people and money was given to them by the boy's relatives. Her uncle was paid for his hospitality to the couple and men of high rank in her lineage were also given a piece of money. This, Ngiraoik explained, was to insure that the husband took good care of the child.

What Ngiraoik did not explain, and what few Palauans can express, was that this payment, along with all the rest that make up the *omulu'ul* system, is an installment on the wife's and the prospective child's services. In effect what the system asserts is that a woman belongs to a different family from her husband and that he must compensate her—which means her kinsmen— for the work that she does for him, a stranger. Her children, like herself, owe their services to her kinsmen, and their loss to their lineage must be paid for by someone, that person being the man who benefits from their services. This leads to a system of financing the careers of children, and the man who has the option is the child's father. He may take the option, release it, or divide it with someone else. Almost always he takes over as a natural expectation of fatherhood.

The financing of a child by its father begins at its birth, or even before that, and ends with its death. Actually, it is usually the father of the father who begins the financing, because he, acting as the financial agent of his son, is obligated to make a payment to his daughter-in-law's financial representative. This is inevitable while the son is a young man. Yet in time he can assume the responsibility for his child as a result of his and his wife's labor for his father's household. In effect, the son labors to buy the interest of his father in his child, and gradually, as he gets older, he begins to manage his child's affairs. He steps into the position held by his father and begins to deal directly with his wife's sponsor, whether this *omulu'ul* partner is her father, her mother's brother, or her brother. Ultimately, of course, as a result of the death of the first two relatives of the wife, a man and his wife's brother assume primary responsibility in a given set of *omulu'ul* exchanges.

While a man may acquire money from his sister's husband as a result of his own labor, and so begin to finance his children and himself, this avenue to independence has its drawbacks. If there are several brothers, none of them may pre-empt the wealth of a common brother-in-law. The Palauans are quick to point out that a woman is equally the sister of each of her brothers; and none of them, least of all a younger brother, is entitled to take sole advantage of the asset she represents. Usually a woman's husband gives a piece of money to her brothers collectively in return for their several services, thus making a division for individual uses impossible. Large pieces of money are always conveyed in this manner, usually to the eldest brother. Lesser pieces, and today American money, are bestowed individually, so that to a limited extent, and in degrees varying with family circumstances, a man can achieve a small measure of independence.

As long as a man is under the domination of an older brother, his position is about what it was while his father lived. The older man has to be appealed to when money is needed for important events in the lives of his nephews and nieces. He acts as his younger brother's representative, except in minor matters, and in all instances when the lineage interests are concerned. Very often men delegate all their functions to their older brothers, and even in old age never act independently. They are, socially speaking, children all of their lives despite their age and domestic status.

Many men must assume only nominal financial control of their children because of their subordinate position in the hierarchy of their matrilineal group. A number of others assume only a partial control in collaboration with their wife's brother. When this happens it is the result of an understanding between the two men. One of them assumes the position of key sponsor and financial manager of a child while the other plays only a secondary role at the wishes and upon the invitation of the other.

If several men stand in eligible relations, they may all sponsor a child and derive benefits from their investments. As we might say colloquially, they may "own a piece" of a child, just as in the United States the managers of singers, actresses, and prize fighters accept partners in their investments in the careers of promising professionals. This analogy is, in fact, a very close one, both from the standpoint of the attitudes involved and of the purposes and techniques of the financial scheme behind the *omulu'ul* system.

When the domestic unit of man, wife, and child is disrupted for any reason, a final accounting must be made to the wife's lineage by the husband's lineage through the financial backers of the couple. These backers may be their fathers, or their mother's brothers, or their brothers, or a combination. The death of any member of the unit—wife, child, or father—precipitates such an accounting. So does divorce.

Here, again, is an indication of the fundamental claim that a man has on his sister and her children, for he, not they, receives the money bestowed on them by their husband and father. It has two parts. One, which has a special name to set it apart, is a payment for the wife's services and is given in her name. It does not matter whether the termination of the marriage is due to the wife's or husband's death, or an agreement between them to end it. In every case, the husband, or his financial agent, pays the man who has financed the affairs of his wife and so has supplied him with food and services for the final feast and for a variable number of occasions antecedent to this event. Some men make only this one payment for accumulated contributions of food and services from their wife's people, but not many can afford this kind of financing. Only a wealthy individual, or one whose investments have been earning better dividends through other channels, will deliberately allow his obligations to accumulate over several years. In most cases it is considered wiser to keep the accounts about even, especially because the final payment, just because it is final, is expected to be a large one. Moreover, the concept of interest enters into the calculation of payments for food. If a man is slow in paying for the food that he receives, he is expected to pay more than if he had made a return in a reasonable time. He is deemed to be using money which he owes, and must therefore expect to pay a premium for the privilege. Consequently, if a man waits until the death of his wife before compensating her brothers for their many contributions, he must expect a demand so heavy that few wish to incur it unless they have some special reason for doing so.

The second part of the financial settlement necessary when a marriage is terminated is called the children's money. This sum is paid by the same individual or individuals who pay the money for the mother, but it does not necessarily go to the same person. It may or may not, depending upon whether the same man is financing the mother and her children. Ultimately, however, the money must be given to the children's mother's brother.

Nominally the children's money belongs to them. It is bestowed upon them by their fathers to be used in their interests. Actually, however, the child never has any control over his patrimony, and sometimes does not see it until he is fully adult and has some need for it. An uncle uses it as he sees fit, and while he is supposed to be held accountable for it by his nieces and nephews, he does very much as he pleases with it and simply tells his wards what he has done, always emphasizing to them that no matter what his decisions have been they were in their best interests. In reality, the children's money is a payment to a man in return for the use of his sister's children by their father. It is essentially no different from the money paid for the wife; both are payments for the services rendered by blood kin to an outsider.

If a man fails to bestow a patrimony, or if he or his heirs are considered to be stingy, his family loses its claim to his children. Their mother's brother asserts his natural right and takes over the management of the children's affairs. The common expression for a man's relinquishment of his children is that he "throws them away." The connotation is that this is a deplorable practice. Men are criticized for it, but not because they thus display a lack of affection for their children. They are censured because they have failed to meet the father ideal, which means that they, or their family, are not able to

meet the financial demands placed upon them. They are insolvent or incompetent or unambitious. They are lacking in pride and are willing to accept relega-
tion to an unimportant social position.

The reasons for "throwing away" children are sometimes those suggested above: some men either do not want to play the financial game or they
are unable to do so. But since many men do not want to admit their failures to
meet the ideal, a common reason, or excuse, lays the blame on the children
themselves. Men defend themselves, often with good reason nowadays, by
saying that their children are worthless and unprincipled; they care nothing
for their fathers, will not work, and are always getting in trouble. Therefore
they "let them go to their mother's people." This statement is significant for
the present discussion because it means that the rejection of children by their
fathers must result in their return to their mother's brother. No one else can
claim them, and their mother's brother has to accept them whether he wants
them or not. He may later make other arrangements for them, but they are his
responsibility, just as they are his prerogatives. He benefits from them if they
turn out well and he loses on them if they do not.

Financial considerations virtually force a man to abandon his children
upon his remarriage. He cannot take his children with him because his new
brother-in-law has no interest in them—no interest because anything that he
gives to his sister in the way of food or service cannot be used in the interests
of her step-children, and hence he cannot receive money in return. Money
earned by them must go to their mother's brother. Consequently, it is usual
for a man to have nothing to do with his children by a previous marriage once
her remarries. The Palauans phrase this pattern of rejection in terms of a
woman's refusal of step-children. They say that children are likely to be mis-
treated by their step-mothers and nobody wants to subject them to such a
situation. Women have some justification for their alleged dislike of step-
children in the common belief that children by previous marriages, if retained
by their fathers, are thereby granted a position of dominance in the household.

The same attitudes account to a large extent for the infrequent occurrence of polygamy. Poor men cannot afford the luxury of two wives, but among
the well-to-do, successive marriages and adopted children are common. For
them the real deterrent to simultaneous marriages is not so much the cost of
maintaining obligations to two families as it is their conflicting demands. Wives
compete for preferential treatment for themselves, their children, and their
siblings. It requires a firm hand to maintain mastery in such a ménage, even
though the wives live separately—and few men have the courage to attempt it.
There are easier ways to accomplish the same purposes.

8

Adding Relatives

PALAUANS are not interested in kinship as such. Their primary concern is with wealth, and kinship for them is a vehicle for its manipulation. They use kinship and seek means to extend artificially its ramifications because it is only within this framework that they can contrive the wealth displays that bring prestige and influence. Kinship is, in fact, phrased in terms, not of friendship or affection or social solidarity, but of status and power. This point of view is well expressed in the Palauan's clichés when he attempts to explain what matrilineal descent means. The most common expression is that a man's sister's children are stronger than his own children. Strength in this context means social and political superiority, and this in turn rests upon the possession of wealth. In other words, the Palauans do not say that a man is more closely allied to his sister's son because of nearness of kinship and consequently that his nephew is the rightful heir to his property; instead it is said that a nephew has a prior and a more forceful claim to a man's property than do his own children.

In the hands of a resourceful individual, a kinship system, like a legal system, can become an effective instrument for the achievement of personal success. One way to use it is to play it up or play it down, insisting on the fulfillment of its obligations or ignoring them, depending upon where the advantage lies. Another way is to extend its operation so that nonrelatives become relatives for all practical purposes. The Palauans are a resourceful people, and they, as individuals, make the most of both opportunities. They emphasize kinship when it pays, and they form profitable ties with fictive fathers, siblings, and children. A foresighted man like Kanai chooses his relatives with care.

Kanai's father was a man from Truk, one of the Micronesian island groups that lie to the east of Palau. Along with other Trukese, Yapese, and Ponapeans he was brought by the Germans to Palau to work in the Angaur phosphate pits. He paid for Kanai's mother in marks and lived with her in good faith but could not marry her in Palauan style because he had no Palauan money. When the Germans were forced out of Micronesia by the Japanese at the outbreak of World War I, Kanai's father was returned to Truk without his wife and five children, the youngest of which was Kanai.

A stranger can live next door to Kanai for months and not be told this part of his life by Kanai or anyone else, even though he may be recording genealogies and daily asking questions about his neighbors. The reason is not that Kanai has anything to hide. He is quite frank about parts of his life that most Americans would prefer to keep to themselves. The point is that the man from Truk has played no significant role in Kanai's life. On the contrary, without money or a place in Palauan society, he has been a liability and would have been no less so had he remained in Palau. Fathers are men for whom one works and who bestow money and land in return. Kanai has had three of these relatives by mutual agreement.

With the departure of Kanai's father, he and his mother and his two brothers and two sisters placed themselves in the care of his mother's brother. They worked for him and assisted him in his exchange obligations for about three years. The children called him *hadam,* my father, and Kanai still refers to him by this term. Then Kanai's mother married a wealthy man, a chief. The children moved into his household with her where they "served" and "prepared for" him. He therefore became *hadam* to the children. When their mother died, he gave a piece of money to their mother's brother for each of them. This chief was Kanai's father at the time of his marriage, and he brought his bride to live in the chief's house. They remained with him for five years, during which time Kanai gave some serious thought to his future. It appeared to him that his prospects for reward in land and money were not very appealing because his father had many other children—some natural, some adopted —and several of them took precedence over Kanai. Furthermore, his father was a chief, which meant that he required a great deal of food and labor to maintain his position. Kanai thought he could better his position, and so had a talk with his first father, the mother's brother who was his real guardian and the holder of his money. He proposed that he put himself at the disposal of his childless sister and her wealthy husband. This was agreed; they made the proposition to Kanai's sister and she persuaded her husband to accept. In this way Kanai became the son of his brother-in-law. It was an especially favorable relationship, for it made him doubly the beneficiary of his brother-in-law and thus gave him an advantage over his brothers and sisters. It has already paid off, for this father has given him three parcels of land which Kanai alleges are his exclusively.

Kanai made another shrewd move when the wife of his mother's brother died during the early part of World War II. Her people had to be paid and they wanted a large piece of money. One about the size of Kanai's would do, but his uncle wanted the consent of all his nephews and nieces before he relinquished it. Kanai came to the family council prepared to release it graciously despite the objections of his brothers and sisters. He says that he wanted to make his "first father" happy. Evidently he succeeded, for his dutiful compliance made the old man weep. Just as importantly, however, he had some misgivings about the future value of Palauan money, especially since the islands were then being hit by American planes beseiging a force of Japanese soldiers on the large island of Babeldaob. Land seemed a much better investment. It is not surprising that Kanai now makes copra on a large piece of land that he claims his uncle left him when he died a few years ago.

It is quite common for men to call their brothers-in-law "father" even though they do not, as Kanai did, live with them as their children. The reason is that a sister's husband takes the place of a father in a most important respect—that is, as a source of money in compensation for service. There is a distinct term for a sister's husband, but the honorific expression, and the one always used in referring to the most influential and wealthy among them, is "father." This usage is so matter-of-fact that it can be misleading. Other filial attitudes and expressions are also extended to brothers-in-law. A man does not speak vulgarly in the presence of his father; neither does he in the presence of his brother-in-law. Deference and submissiveness are due a father as they are due a brother-in-law. As the Palauan sees it, just as a father substitutes for a mother's brother in the game of financing, so the sister's husband ultimately substitutes for the father. The three sets of relationships are not the same, but the emphasis is on source of income, and the sister's husband is in the last analysis the source of the source, the father of the father.

In cases like Kanai's, adults assume the role of children and cultivate it with selected fathers. The relationship is not quite like that of an adopted child. The Palauans speak of a man such as Kanai as "being with" his stepfather or his brother-in-law. This is the same term that is used for trial adoptions—that is, those instances when a child lives with his proposed foster parents for a probationary period during which he proves his worth as a financial investment. The trial is undertaken voluntarily by the child's father with the understanding that the foster father may terminate it without obligation. The same idea is often expressed with respect to the real father. Children cannot "belong" to their father's clan, but ideally they should "be with" it until he dies. Ordinarily they will, if they turn out well; but as they grow older their relationship to him is not so different from that of a fictive father.

Parents seek children for much the same reason that men seek parents. Although there are cases in which couples take the children of other people because of sentimental reasons, and still others in which people become emotionally attached to their foster children, an ever-present motivation, and the most common primary and sufficient reason for a child being adopted, is that the change in his sponsorship does one of three things. It relieves a financial strain on his parents; or it opens up new opportunities for material benefit for himself or his uncle; or it secures an additional advantage for his foster parents. All of these ends may, of course, be served at the same time so that everyone concerned makes a financial gain.

Often parents do not want to let their child go but find themselves in a position such that the choice is not entirely theirs. It may be that the wife's

brother or her uncle is childless, or he may be wealthy and with too few dependents to satisfy his ambitions. Similarly, if a man's older brother, or his
father, or his sister's husband, or his wife's father is in need of dependents to
give full play to his aspirations, he might find himself obliged as a father to
accede to their demands. In that event, and quite apart from the practical sense
he is expected to show in yielding, a man can console himself with the thought
that his children's interests may better be served if he allows them to become
the protégés of more influential and wealthy men.

Adopted children always know who their real parents are, for there
is no effort made to conceal this fact from them. Indeed, concealment would
not be feasible because the real father retains the privilege of using the patrimony of his children that comes from their foster father. Just as a woman's
father may take the patrimony of her children if he wishes to obligate himself
to pay it and the interest due on it to their mother's brother at some future
time, so may a natural father use the money paid by the step-father of his
children. Ultimately the patrimony of his children, paid by their step-father,
must go to their mother's brother; but their father can, so to speak, intercept
it and turn it to his advantage by agreement with his brother-in-law. Some
men do not want to take advantage of this privilege, because they do not
need the money, or because the interest they must pay is too high, or because
they have no social ambitions.

A child may be adopted several times. Each time an adoption is terminated there must be a payment of money for the child. No man is obligated
to make such a settlement more than once, but each individual who enters into
the father relationship with the child has at some time to make a settlement
upon him. The step-father assumes the responsibility for this when either
he or the child dies. If a child survives the first adoption, he may be taken by
a third man who likewise obligates himself to make a settlement under the
same circumstances. In all cases, the person who eventually receives all of the
payments is the child's mother's brother. Hence it is evident that this individual
is not averse to seeing his nephew or niece adopted as many times as possible.
It is not considered good taste to openly admit this, at least to an outsider,
but it is an accepted attitude among the Palauans themselves. An adoption is
rarely regarded as a permanent attachment between a child and its foster
parents. This is because children are often adopted more than once and because
they can at any time leave their foster parents and return to their real fathers.
However, if a child leaves without the consent of the foster parents, he gets no
money from them nor does his father. On the other hand, if foster parents
send their adopted children away, they must make a property settlement on
them.

Adoptions are almost always within the limits of what the Palauan
considers to be the close family group. Typically, a woman adopts her brother's
child. This pattern promotes the interests of the child's father by fitting the
adoption into the *omulu'ul* scheme. By it a father maneuvers himself into a
position such that he will be able to receive money on his child's account from
his brother-in-law instead of having to expend it. Through this mechanism he

becomes virtually the mother's brother of his child; and while this is a fictional relationship, it nonetheless has its advantages.

The idea behind adoption is always to place the control of children in the hands of some man who is outside their family so that they will provide a source of money for their maternal male kin. This is just what happens when the father of a child supports it and assumes financial responsibility for it. The mother's brother can thereby ply the father with food and increase the returns on the child. In this way, the uncle can set the pace for the exchanges by providing his sister's husband with as much food and service as he wishes, using the child's career as an excuse for this artificial stimulation. When the father allows his child to be adopted, he wants to be placed in the same position himself. Consequently, the obvious thing to do is to allow the child to be adopted by his sister's husband. The money which comes to him as a result of this arrangement must be ultimately paid to his wife's brother, the mother's brother of the child, but he can have the use of it indefinitely.

Children are not consulted about these dealings. They are expected to accede to the wishes of their parents and to change their attitudes and their behaviors toward their parents along with the shift in their fortunes. Parents are expected to be equally objective about their children and to take their changes of status as a matter of course. This is the ideal attitude and the one which is normally in evidence. There are, however, suggestions that although people acquiesce to the demands of custom, they are not always happy about it. These contrary sentiments are never overtly expressed except in individual cases and in unguarded moments. The conventional response to questioning about attitudes on this matter are statements to the effect that one must naturally grant the request of a sister or a brother or some other relative to take possession of one's child because it is obviously well intentioned. More-over, it is the duty of a person to talk his or her spouse into the proposal on behalf of their blood relatives. It is only when the subject is approached obliquely that evidences of feelings of reluctance appear.

The *omulu'ul* system is also used to establish fictive sibling relation-ships. A man can establish such a relationship with another man or woman by aiding them in the way that he would aid his real brother or sister. This device produces a "tied relationship." It is an extension of the pattern for adopting children and is an equally common phenomenon—so common that if two people assist each other economically, there is a tendency to consider their desire to establish a kinship bond a foregone conclusion.

It is very easy for two individuals to establish such a fictional kinship bond between them. It can develop gradually over the space of several years, or it can be accomplished more or less formally, beginning on a certain date. Two people may become associated in this way during their lifetimes and the affiliation can end with the death of either of them. On the other hand, it is equally common for their descendants to assume the obligations that they have established and carry on the relationship indefinitely through generations. As a result of two men establishing their brotherhood in this fashion, an entire lineage or a clan becomes virtually absorbed in another, especially if one has been considerably reduced in numbers, or when the opportunity for social advancement within it becomes restricted. Under such circumstances the head of the dwindling lineage or clan will unite in a tied relationship with a prominent individual of another family and thereby take his heirs into an arena of greater opportunity for himself and for them.

The tied relationship can be established not only between individuals of the same generation but can also exist between an adult and a child. What actually happens in the case of a father taking his children into his clan is that a tied relationship is established between him and them and the members of his maternal group. Again, this is a reciprocal relationship operating under the *omulu'ul* system, but there is in this instance the feeling of blood kinship as well.

When in the course of time several clans have been united in a tied relationship, the result is a grouping which is called the *kleblil*. There are numerous alliances of this sort and frequently one clan or one lineage is tied to several others in a way that is quite confusing unless one has clearly in mind the basis of the relationship. It is because of this that men may assume positions of first importance in a clan even though it is impossible to trace any genealogical connection between them and the members of the clan of which they assume leadership. No kinship exists between the chiefs of some of the most important clans in Palau and the real members of those clans. Commonly the office of chieftainship passes completely outside the clan when no one within it is immediately eligible because of age or other qualifications and goes to a prominent individual within the *kleblil*. Again, the explanation is quite reasonable to the Palauan because real kinship is less important to him than the bonds that are established through service and economic obligations. Consequently, an individual who has served a group well and is in a position to represent its financial interests in an outstanding way is a more likely candidate for leadership than someone claiming mere blood kinship.

When Sat was a school boy he visited Angaur and there became acquainted with a little girl much younger than himself. He liked to play with her, often looked after her, and she began to call him her big brother. He did not stay very long in Angaur, and it was some time before he saw the girl again. In the years that followed he saw her intermittently and she recalled on those occasions their earlier friendship and continued to refer to him as her brother. He thought nothing of this, and even forgot about the girl until just before the last war when they met again while she and her father were visiting relatives in his district. Upon that occasion she brought some presents for him that she had bought in Angaur. Then, during the war she and many other refugees from the more exposed parts of Palau lived in the hills of Sat's district. By this time Sat had developed a big-brother interest in her and told his wife to see to it that the girl was provided with food. Sat's wife did this from time to time during the war, after which the girl returned to her home in Angaur. She was married shortly before this and now has two small children.

Recently Sat has begun to realize a return on his investment in his adopted sister. Lately he again visited Angaur and took several baskets of taro and several stalks of bananas to give to the girl and her husband. This gift served to point up the relationship existing between them and to bring it to the attention of the girl's husband. On another visit to Angaur Sat again took food to his adopted sister. While he was there, her husband, helped by his relatives, presented Sat with $100. That exchange made the two men brothers-in-law under the *omulu'ul* system. Sat said that he did not want the $100, and tried to refuse it, saying that he had no need of it just then. His newly acquired brother-in-law insisted that he take at least a part of it, and he was obliged to accept $50, "just to spend in having a good time" during his visit to Angaur. Now the girl is just like one of Sat's real sisters, except that there is no feeling of blood relationship. This arrangement also gives Sat the advantage of being an older brother. With respect to his real family he is the youngest child, an unfortunate situation for an ambitious man.

The tied relationship is the explanation for the otherwise puzzling statement that a person is "a little bit inside" of a particular clan. There can be degrees of kinship in this sense because there are degrees of nearness to the principals who have established a fictional brotherhood. Keta and his sisters belong to the clan of their mother. So did their elder brother, but he left it to join their father's clan to serve as its chief. But he is still their brother and so they are a little bit inside their father's clan, too. This means that they must help its members, but not so much as those who are born in it.

9

Commanding Respect

I N PALAU, age in itself commands respect, but so does success; and often these two qualifications for esteem and authority do not coincide. In fact, in the majority of individual cases there is some discrepancy.

Men 35 years old always treat their elders, including women, very respectfully. A young man will listen to the advice of an old woman most attentively and will take her scolding without a reply, even though she is not related to him. Young people of both sexes are taught to defer to old women as well as to old men, and they do so in all outward respects even though sometimes there can be no doubt that they feel imposed upon. It appears that they more sincerely respect old women than old men, probably because they are constantly being ordered about by the latter. On all formal occasions, such as those upon which food and money are transferred, the oldest women have privileges, although they are minor, that are denied the young men. They are in their turn, of course, subordinated to the older men, and even in individual instances to men who are not their equals in age. The latter circumstance comes about as the result of some younger men possessing a title, and it is one of those complications resulting from a conflict of principles from which no cultural system is entirely free.

There are two levels of leadership and two classes of titles conferred on men accepted as chiefs. One class acknowledges authority only within a clan, the other within a community at large, whether it be a village, a district, or a combination of districts. Each local segment of a clan owns the right to a title for its leader that is hereditary in the maternal line. There is a companion title for the ranking woman of the clan. Titles of this character grant authority only within an extended household or a combination of households of maternal relatives.

Some men who are clan leaders and consequently hold clan titles have additional titles which qualify them to sit on village or district councils and to exercise authority beyond their kin group. Only these men are properly called *rupaks*. Their political titles are quite distinct from their clan titles, although they too are inherited in the maternal line. Companion female titles give their bearers authority over women's affairs in the community. Ideally a man and his sister hold companion titles.

Rupaks once had heavy responsibilities and authoritarian power. In their heyday they had the right to requisition food and to impose fines on the members of their village or district. They made rules and sat in judgment on offenders. They conscripted service for their benefit and that of the community. They were priests as well as secular leaders with supposed supernatural power to bolster and sanction their pre-emptory decrees. They expected to be informed of all that happened within their jurisdictions and did not hesitate to summon a person to give an accounting of his intentions or behavior. They were present at all public and important family affairs, acting as advisors and record keepers. Visitors waited to be received by them to explain the purpose of their visit and were officially dispatched at its conclusion. Strangers did not enter a district unless escorted by a chief or his known representative. Titled men of all degrees were granted outward gestures of respect. No common person could approach them upright; lesser men stepped off the trail and bowed low as they passed; they were always addressed in a low voice at close range, never hailed.

All of these acknowledgments of high rank have lessened under foreign rule. Nevertheless, in spite of the curtailment of chiefly power, a great deal of respect is still accorded the holder of a title. This is because titles in themselves are venerated. They are revered because of their histories and the personalities of their bearers in the past. They are distinct from the men who are invested with them, for certain rights and duties are automatically linked with them. Moreover, so great is the regard for them that they are imbued with something of a personality of their own. Even now their assumption is an inspiration, and very often it brings a startling transformation in the behavior of the man who acquires it.

For these reasons a man is given the respect associated with a title, regardless of his age. Normally, titles are not bestowed upon young men, and in no case may a very young man, say of age 20, assume an important clan title. However, it must inevitably happen that some men with high-ranking titles are younger than some other men either with or without titles. This poses a problem, and the solution to it depends upon the particular circumstances involved. When there is no major difference between titles, age takes precedence and becomes more important than title rating. A comparatively young man with a high-ranking title will, if he is wise, remain quiet in councils and let himself be guided by the advice of older men who are associated with him. Even then he may be resented and his decisions contested. He is in a self-contradictory position, for, ideally, middle or late age and title should go together.

For the same reason, old men without titles are placed in an uncomfortable position, for a title is the symbol of success. It is expected that in addition to growing old, a man should also engage in the financial game of manipu-

lating the wealth of as many people as possible. The less a man has engaged
in these activities the less important he is with respect to someone else of his
own age who has undertaken a career of this sort and earned a title. Since
not everyone is in a position to participate in the game and still others have
no taste for it, there is a category of old men without formal social standing.
They are called *wogel sahal,* which means, simply, aged men. They are men
who have passed the active years of their lives without having made a name
for themselves.

The position of the *wogel sahal* is therefore an ambiguous, and sometimes a pathetic, one. They tend to take themselves more seriously than do
other members of the society. The titled men give them little consideration and
are rather abrupt with them on formal occasions since they regard them as
incompetents and failures. Young people treat them with outward consideration but with inward impatience because young men can look forward to a
time when they will have achieved a position superior to them. They, like the
young chief, are in a contradictory position, but for opposite reasons.

The difficulty is that the Palauan theory of social existence does not
fit the facts of life. The theory is that with advancing age a man assumes a
title and engages in the praiseworthy manipulation of his family's wealth.
This does happen, but obviously it cannot happen to every man. The happy
situation results when the ideal and the real coincide—when a titled man is
an elderly man and vice-versa. If everyone died at the same age, the Palauan
system would work out happily for most people, because then money and authority would usually be vested in the eldest males and would devolve on their
younger brothers, then on their nephews, as they passed away. As it is, some
men live longer than their younger brothers and even their sons and nephews,
so that the latter never get a chance to match their age with authority and
respect.

There is another category of old men other than those who have never
been the head of a lineage or a clan or held a political title. They are the men
who have once been important but are no longer so. Palauan reputations are
based upon present activity, not on the memory of past glory. A man cannot
rest on his laurels; there are too many others who want to make a name for
themselves. Some elderly men, grown too infirm or slow witted to maintain the
pace, voluntarily retire in favor of their heirs. Others cannot face this abrupt
step into limbo and so cling to their positions long after they are capable of
maintaining them. The delay cannot go on indefinitely, however, and to such
men one of two fates is in store. Either they retain their position in name only,
being gradually elbowed to the sidelines by more vigorous men; or their title
is taken from them by another man with the consent of his dependents or by a
coup d'état supported by the other titled men.

Among the retired men, then, there are embittered ones as well as those
who are resigned to a neglected old age. Many of the former leave their districts to live elsewhere, at times continuing to claim their former rights and
denouncing the pretenders to their titles. Such intransigence can be effective.
There is at the present time, for example, an ousted chief of one district who

when he voluntarily exiled himself took with him the Palauan money that he possessed by reason of his title. He holds it, unable to use it, but also preventing its use by his successor. Long ago this dilemma would have been resolved by a war. Today there is no agreed upon way to deal with it.

Men who have quietly retired or who have never met the challenge of leadership inevitably slip into association with women and children because there is no other provision for them. In the past, membership in a club and the existence of a meeting place helped to set such men apart and created an *esprit de corps* even though they held a relatively unimportant position. With the club organization gone they have little to do and no place to go except home. There they are to be found, talking with wives and with whoever may drop in. To a large extent they remain silent except when something in conversation harks back to their youth, and even then they speak with less assurance than they once did. In general they are mild and unassuming, sometimes scarcely noticeable as they sit quietly in a darkened corner of their house.

It is in these declining years that old men are likely to form attachments with the very young, the children of their sons and daughters, adopted and real. The affection is genuine, though seldom evidenced by a display of emotion. The relationship can develop into a touching companionship when the child is for some reason not quite normal. Nias is a man of 60 who, though in line for the assumption of a title, voluntarily let the honor bypass him 20 years ago. He is mild mannered and kindly and completely devoted to his crippled grandson, aged seven. Glimpses of them playing around the fringes of life in the village leave an indelible memory: the old man poling the boy on a bamboo raft in the quiet lagoon; the two of them watching young men at work, or strolling hand in hand down the village street.

Old men are also drawn into association with women as a result of their conversion to Christianity. A few of them among the Protestants serve as village pastors, leading the congregation in prayers and in the singing of hymns. Usually, though, the leaders, as well as the leaders among the Catholic converts, are chiefs. The rest of the church-going membership is typically composed of elderly men without authority, women of all ages, and children. The gap made by the absence of young men is noticeable in almost all congregations, and it does not seem to be a temporary or an accidental feature. Christianity came to the islands long ago and its missionaries have labored patiently and persistently to bring Palauans of all classes and ages into the church. Active young men shy away, but as they approach the end of their lives many return to the faith they left earlier or accept it for the first time. Evidently its consolation for mundane failures and its promise of a future fill a void.

Not all aged men turn to Christianity any more than do all women and children. Neither are all converts failures and defeated men. Yet it is apparent that it offers to those who are such a place and a recognition of their individual worth which is denied them by the system into which they were born. They are seldom active participants in church services or in the meetings held for the religious instruction of children. Usually they let the women take the lead in singing, praying, and catechizing while they remain in the background, passively and mutely following the outward forms of participation. In this as in native ceremonials, women are the main protagonists and the keepers of public ritual.

As is only natural, old people are the followers of the ways of their youth insofar as there is an effort to retain them at all. They are the supporters of the *omulu'ul* system against the almost solid opposition of the younger men. The latter believe themselves to be victimized by an outmoded system which exploits their abilities for the benefit of the oldsters who have a vested interest in it. In this, however, there is no clear-cut division between the generations. Young as well as old women cling to the exchanges because they reinforce kin-group loyalties and give a wife the concern and protection that she does not receive from her husband. Her brothers are her guardians and protectors. Her husband might favor a shift to the independence of the family unit; but of this she has no assurance and not a little to cause her to have misgivings. Husbandly behavior has not markedly changed with the trend toward economic individualism.

All that remains of the ancient arts, skills, and lore is preserved in the hands and minds of the older members of the community. Once in awhile a gray-haired breech-clouted man can be seen slowly adzing a taro dish out of a block of wood or knotting a tough string to make a fish net, using toes as well as fingers to keep the string taut. Or near the beach on the edge of the village there may be a solitary canoe maker, chopping and sawing a hull out of the trunk of a tree.

In Palau, as in other lands, everything becomes harder to do as one gets older, from climbing trees to getting married. Daob, trying to take his third wife, had reason to complain about this and in particular about the Palauan customs which thwarted him. As well as he could estimate his age at the time, he was around 60. He was poor with no close relatives except a married son and a daughter for whom he was trying to make a match so that he could get enough money to get married himself. That he needed a strong woman to work for him was obvious to any eligible woman, as was the fact that he did not have long to live. The latter consideration would not have mattered had he been wealthy; in fact, it would have been an advantage to his bride's people, for they would have realized a quick return on their services to him at his death. Under the circumstances, his prospects were not good unless he could raise more money than would be expected of him as a young man who would be likely to make payments over many years.

Daob did not get a wife, and as it turned out that did not matter. Shortly after his daughter was married he was found dead in the little house where he lived alone. The stir that this event created was in marked contrast to his ineffectiveness in life. It was a striking revelation of the underlying network of ultimate obligations which hold Palauan society together. Daob, who in life had only two visible relatives and not many more friends, suddenly was the center of attention for most people in the village, the activator of a dynamic system of social and ritual demands. His body was found early in the morning, and within an hour the word had been spread far beyond his neighborhood and his village. Men who had scarcely been recognized as his relatives while he lived congregated in the yard in the front of his house, there to be joined by the chiefs of the village and beyond. All morning they continued to straggle in from near and distant places. Women who were in some way responsible for food for the occasion, either through clan connections with the dead man or through their husbands, set off for their fields immediately. The entire village seemed mysteriously alive with people, first going in all directions, later converging on the scene of the funeral.

The corpse had been taken to the house of the head man of Daob's clan. It lay on a mat on the floor near one wall, dressed in its "best": shirt, trousers, socks, and shoes never worn in life and donated for the occasion by a relative. It had been washed with a heavily scented soap, in place of the old preparation of aromatic leaves, and its lips smeared with lipstick, a modern substitute for betel juice. A faded army cap lay on the pillow at one side of the head; on the other was a handbag containing the cherished possessions that were to accompany the corpse to the grave.

As the mourning women arrived to take their places around the corpse, the younger ones handed Daob's clan "mother" a few yards of dress goods; the older ones gave her finely made mats. These goods were to be used to reward the rest of the women for the food they brought and for their preparation of it. The mourners arrived one by one over the period of an hour. Some of them wept and brought tears to the eyes of the rest as they approached the body. Between their arrivals there were muted conversations among those already present and among the detached cluster of men. Betel nut was sent for and distributed by the head of the house to all persons in the room. A coffin maker was at work in the yard in the midst of a crowd of squatting men who gave advice. At one point he passed a tape measure in the window, asking one of the women to measure the corpse. Later he returned to ask for some of the dress goods with which to line the coffin.

By that time it was 3 o'clock and everyone was hungry. The grave diggers returned about then and food was served. It was an unpretentious repast consisting of cold fish and taro and weak tea. The mourning women were served where they sat around the corpse; the chiefs and other important men retired to an adjacent house, and the common men ate in the yard. Desultory conversation went on until 5 o'clock when the clan head directed that the coffin be taken in the house and the corpse placed in it. This was the final farewell, and before the lid was placed on the coffin the women hovered over it wailing loudly, crying again and again "What are you doing? Why must it be so?"

When the women's cries subsided, all the mourners and some of the men recited a kind of litany called a "Catholic prayer." After that there was a long and uneventful wait that was finally ended when the chief pointed out that it was getting late, that the sun was setting. The lid was placed on the coffin and it was brought outside. There it was placed in a rope cradle and slung on two poles. Four men carried it to the cemetery on the hillside above the village that has been the burying place for all families since the Germans forbade interment on ancestral home sites. None of the women came out of the house; those who sat around the corpse—the official mourners—had to seclude themselves for five days, doing nothing, being served by the rest of the women. There was no last-minute demonstration of grief, and only the pall bearers accompanied the body to the grave.

The property settlement was arranged late that evening after another and more elaborate meal. It followed the funeral immediately, for everyone wanted to do what had to be done and go home. For more important people, a longer interval would have elapsed and more food and money would have changed hands. Long ago, the entire village or district would have gone into mourning for a high-ranking chief, 100 days for his immediate relatives, 25 days for everyone. The bodies of lesser men would have lain in state for five days, resting on a platform for everyone to see. There would have been grave watches, repeated mourning rites, and many feasts. With time, however, there has been a leveling of these ritualistic expressions of loss, thus leaving proportionately less observance to mark the passing of a common man.

10

Being Different

MEN LIKE DAOB inevitably come to the attention of a close observer of village life, for they are undoubtedly a significant part of it. They may affect it little or not at all, but their deviations and failures are significant for an appreciation of the conformance and successes of others. They are conspicuous because they throw into relief the salient features of the life around them, a spectacle in which they figure as observers rather than participants. Their role is not entirely passive; often they are outspoken skeptics and critics. Whatever their peculiarities may be, it is important to appreciate that there are deviant personalities in Palau, if for no other reason than to offset the prevalent opinion that "primitive" societies are homogeneous entities, solid blocks of colorless conformers. Some Palauans are no different from some Americans in that they do not like some of the most cherished customs of their associates.

Very often the presence of a stranger, ignorant or unbiased by native attitudes, acts as a kind of catalyst that precipitates deviant individuals out of the mass. Many are drawn to him, seeking company more congenial than that of their fellows, and not infrequently hoping thereby to gain some personal advantage. Some thrust themselves abruptly and boldly into the spotlight of attention. Others emerge only gradually, at first seen through the eyes of their detractors, later as personalities in their own right. Still others are too proud to bend a knee to anyone, and if they expose themselves to a stranger at all it will be only at his insistence.

Daob was about 15 when a German entymologist came to Palau to collect specimens. He needed a helper, and since Daob spoke a little German he was offered the job. His father was dead and he did not like his uncle, and he was therefore glad to accept the opportunity to serve as houseboy, bearer, and guide for the scientist. As they moved from place to place in Palau, Daob was impressed with the respect with which his employer was treated and was able to turn some of this to his own advantage. He developed a great admiration for the scientist's knowledge and apparently assimilated his unsympathetic view of Palauan life. Daob talked a great deal about his mentor while he worked for him and after he left the islands. This aggravated his already strained relations with his friends and they began contemptuously to call him "Herr Professor," the only name by which the scientist was known. The nickname stuck and it was still used until the time of his death, even by people who corrupted its pronunciation and did not know what it meant.

There was every reason why the name and its overtones of derision were retained, for Daob became progressively more estranged from Palauan society as time went on. He was not a good "lineage man" and he had many quarrels with his uncle. He was not a good husband and lost two wives in divorce. He was able to take care of only two of his five children. The change from German to Japanese rule was a shock to him, for he could not make an adjustment to the new order. Either he disliked the Japanese, or they him, or both, for he had only hateful memories of them. The coming of the Americans offered him another chance to identify himself with what he regarded as a superior people.

The opportunity became quite real a few months before he died when two American anthropologists came to live in a village near his. Very early in their stay he came bearing little gifts along with cast-off foreign objects— a flashlight, an air rifle, a pair of scissors—asking for help in repairing them. Like every other visitor, he knew that he could usually count on a cigarette from his hosts, but most of all he wanted to talk. He always appeared when no other Palauan was present and always found an opportunity to scoff at them and at Palauan customs. A few weeks before he died, he pleaded to be taken to Guam when the Americans left. He said he thought he had a friend living there.

Klegman was born under the Japanese regime and, unlike Daob, spent the happiest years of his life while it lasted. He went through a village school and was chosen for training in animal husbandry on a station near Koror. He lived there for twelve years with a Japanese family. He now lives in his native village where he is one of three school teachers. He is married, has no children of his own, and refuses to adopt one. He is a large man with a muscular appearance that seems out of keeping with his sensitive tastes and delicate mannerisms. He of all Palauans carries a handkerchief, usually a clean one, and uses it daintily. He is anxiety ridden, uncertain of himself, fearful of making a mistake or of being outclassed by the other teachers. He carries a chip on his shoulder and is constantly bickering with his associates about some alleged slight or an interpretation contrary to his own. He knows the Japanese language better than he knows Palauan and for this reason he avoids any situation which might expose his ignorance of Palauan idioms or vocabulary refinements—what Palauans call "inside talk." He is not alone in this insecurity, but he suffers most from it. He hopes and believes that the Palauan language is on its way out. He says that when the old people die it will fade away with them. This, however, gives him cause for further worry, for Japanese is even more certainly a useless investment. Hence his eagerness to learn English and to surpass others with the same ambition.

It was due mainly to this incentive that he became a persistent caller at the house of the anthropologists. For awhile he appeared every evening and stayed very late. He brought with him a Japanese-English dictionary out of which he chose Japanese words, the English meaning of which he wanted to know. Most of them were abstract terms and many of them unconsciously exposed some of his personal problems: "slander," "infamy," "envy," "compatability," "injustice." He was a welcome visitor, for the Americans were as eager to learn Palauan as he was to learn English, but the advantage was on his side. Working through a dictionary slowed the learning process and made its content academic. This pleased him, for it gave him a precious vocabulary with which he could awe and confound the other teachers. There was another purpose behind the long, regular, nightly sessions. He adopted a proprietary attitude toward the two Americans. They were his means of establishing a monopoly on the local source of English. He resented and thrust aside any attempt to infringe on it by others; and when the Americans refused to recognize it he became moody and uncommunicative.

Klegman's attitude toward Palau faithfully mirrored his Japanese training. From a Japanese anthropologist he learned to view Palauan culture somewhat objectively and to debunk its folklore; pigs and chickens were not indigenous as most Palauans thought, but had been introduced to the islands from Malaya; fish spears were not invented by the Palauans, but had come from the Philippines; "native" money was introduced by the Portuguese and was not brought down from the sky as legend told; the terraced mountainsides and stone ruins that are scattered around the islands were not the work of gods or supermen. From his many other Japanese associations he came to deplore or be ashamed of certain customs. He absorbed as completely as any Palauan male the Japanese distaste for Palauan nakedness. He looked upon breech cloths as symbols of backwardness and pointed to the Yapese as an example of a people too low in the human scale ever to rise above the use of them. The *omulu'ul* system was barbaric and had, he said, been forbidden by the Japanese. Fortunately in his capacity as a teacher he was exempted from most of its demands as well as those of community service. Not only were these customs bad; so were the Palauans themselves. They were born with a streak of meanness, treachery, and deception.

One of Klegman's pupils ran afoul of his ambition and was summarily dismissed from school. Jacob, the pupil, was older than most of his classmates and was not as pliant as they were. Like Klegman, he had lived with a Japanese family in Koror after his mother died, but, unlike Klegman, he had not absorbed their viewpoint, perhaps because his residence with them was shorter, or perhaps because it did not appeal to him. In any event, his association with the family helped to disassociate him from Palauan life in general. At the time the two Americans arrived in his village he was apparently seeking a solution to this problem. In the wake of the war he had made himself useful around the camps of American service personnel in Koror and had picked up a little English, mostly bad. Later he had returned to his village, where he lived with his father and an older brother and sister. He did not like school. Furthermore, he distrusted Klegman whose insecurity he sensed and aggravated by his own urge to sophistication. He too wanted to learn English and this led him to spend much time at the house of the Americans, observing them, listening to them, puzzling over pictures in illustrated magazines.

These contacts gave him ideas which he put into effect to the best of his understanding and ability. As so often happens in such cases of incomplete communication, the results were bizarre if not pathetic efforts at imitation. One day he appeared wanting his picture taken. His kinky hair was plastered flat with a heavy application of odorous palmade and he was garbed in a style that befitted his conception of a dashing young Palauan-American: white shorts, long rubber boots, colored glasses, and a long watch chain draping down to the hem of his shorts. When asked what background he preferred, he rejected the front of his own home as too shabby and chose the school building as a symbol of his ambition.

After he was no longer permitted to attend school he came to ask the anthropologists if he could work for them. They were not living in a style to support or even use a houseboy to advantage, but they agreed to let him have the run of the house during the day, doing what he thought might be useful in return for what he got out of the association. He could not cook, clean, or wash, for these things were not a part of a man's job. Before long, an opportunity came for him to join a geologist working out of headquarters in Koror. Finally, through his contacts with Americans, he was able to go to Guam and from there to the United States. He has not returned to Palau and probably will not.

Jacob acquired his distaste for Palau naturally. His father, Shiro, was an individualist, too. The only Palauan things about him were as distinctive of him as they were generically Palauan: a bright red breech cloth, a fierce pride, an extraordinary skill as a turtle fisherman. He was also the only artisan working in iron in his district, and one of the very few in the islands. He was industrious and deplored all of the time wasted by others in gossiping and scheming for position. He was especially contemptuous of titled men, for they spent much of their time bargaining for advantage—talking instead of working for a living. From these activities he abstained almost completely. He, more than anyone else, criticized the chiefs for their labor levies on the people and for their cash demands on their dependents, pointing out that they were abusing their traditional prerogatives. The latter, he said, should no longer be recognized. Before their power was overridden by alien governments, they had been entitled to make money and labor demands on their subordinates because they gave protection and assistance in return for it. Now this compensation was gone and they had no real authority, yet they expected to be supported as in the past. Their scheming to get American money was galling because they siphoned it off from the men who worked for it. In addition to all this, they were incompetent. They could not plan a community project efficiently.

Shiro spent most of his time at home. He was devoted to his children and refused to consider remarriage, for that would have meant letting them go to someone else. He held to this decision even though it worked a hardship on him and his family. His youngest daughter was a school girl, too young to do the most strenuous part of the work in the taro fields. She had two married sisters who helped her when they could. One was a neighbor married to a man with many of the same aversions to Palauan culture as his father-in-law. He was strongly opposed to adoption and to *omulu'ul* and sympathized with his wife's efforts to supply her family with food. The third daughter lived in another district. She visited her father twice each year to help her sisters maintain their taro fields. But without a woman in the house there was less taro and more manioc and sweet potatoes in the daily fare of this family than is customary. In compensation there was more rice and a more regular supply of fish.

Shiro was not an open rebel. He did not defy authority; he simply evaded it. He did not expect or want to be recognized, as did Daob. He was never seen walking around the village calling on people or sitting at a gathering. His alienation from Palauan custom had led him to cast his lot with the Japanese, and he was one of a very few highly selected Palauans to be taken to Japan on an indoctrination tour. The fortunes of war had not worked to his advantage, but he was not embittered. Realistically he resigned himself to a thwarted career and resolved to encourage his son to affiliate himself with the new order and to succeed where he had failed. He accepted Jacob's dismissal from school and prompted him to ask for work with the Americans, although he remained detached from them as well as from the Palauans. He never visited the anthropologists and asked no favors from them. He was friendly and talkative when they called on him, but he never relaxed his poise and dignity. He could have been a proud and fearsome warrior had he lived a century earlier.

Shiro and his fellow dissenters were different because they chose to be. Alleman was different because he could not help it. Until the last war he was a typically inconspicuous young man playing the minor role for which he seemed destined by birth and family circumstances. The stress of privation during the siege of Babeldaob, the loss of relatives, and the shock of bombs and gunfire apparently disturbed his contact with reality. He developed a mild megalomania and periodically he imagined that the war was still on and that he was a Japanese security officer. Ordinarily his conception of himself as a chief was harmless and could be easily ignored. Like a chief, he was not expected to work. He spent most of his time calling from house to house, keeping in touch with what was going on. He assumed a head man's prerogatives of being supplied with betel, tobacco, and food, of inquiring into the affairs of others, and of directing whatever operation might be in progress. Occasionally he spoke coherently; usually, though, he jabbered unintelligently. Palauans say that he does not speak Palauan. Most people are tolerant of his imperious manner and his brusque utterances, indulging him when it is convenient, ignoring him when he is too unreasonable. Titled men overlook his transgression on their domain when they can, although they often have to dismiss him from their deliberations or ask him to be quiet when he tries to interject his views. Everyone laughs at him at times, but the young people go out of their way to make sport of him. Pretending to take him seriously, they tease him unmercifully. When he attempts to tell them what to do, they listen attentively and then ask him to demonstrate.

At times Alleman has to be explained to strangers. Unless diverted or ordered to be off, he confronts them with a stern countenance and a staccato gibberish, evidently intent on determining their business. If he is not restrained, he is likely to go through their baggage, seeking no one knows what. Once he strode boldly to the place where several Americans were sitting on a bench in the schoolyard and sharply turned up their feet and inspected the soles of their shoes. He then proceeded to denounce them, as well as could be determined, for being peeping toms. This was the interpretation, at least, of the embarrassed constable whom he summoned. It appeared that, for reasons known only to Alleman, his suspicions had been aroused by shoeprints that he had observed around one of the houses that morning.

Ardial was another man who lived in a world of his own, though in retrospect it has become more comprehensible to those who tell his story. He lived in Ngarard before the Germans arrived in the islands, but according to his believers he knew that they were coming and that many other wonders would occur. At the time, people thought he was crazy, but now they know that he was in communication with some god and was able to foresee future events. Most of what he said and did took on meaning only in the light of later occurrences, and doubtless many of the things attributed to him have been consciously or unconsciously interpolated or embroidered to substantiate the theme of his legend.

It is said of Ardial that he began to wear white trousers, shirts, and a hat at a time when none of the Ngarard people had heard of such things. He predicted that in time all Palauans would be wearing these garments. He also began to plant coconuts and told others that they must get accustomed to the idea because soon they must all do it. This prophecy was borne out later, when the Germans required each Palauan male to plant a quota. Ardial also made a small model of a house in the European style, never before known in Palau, and equipped it with chairs and tables, saying that this was coming to the islands. He put a flag pole in front of it bearing a white flag with red and blue bars on it. He also put flags on the tops of the highest hills without giving any explanation beyond saying that they should be there. He scribbled signs on small boards which he posted around the countryside on trees. He told the people to study these markings for they, too, represented something with which the Palauans would one day be familiar. Seemingly these scribblings were not alphabetical symbols but mere marks. Yet today people say that they were writing. Some even claim that they were Japanese characters.

In any case, they indicated a foreknowledge of the day when the Palauans would be going to school.

People were afraid of Ardial while he lived and did not question him closely about the meaning of his acts. Most scoffed at him or ignored him completely. Reflecting on this, some Palauans nowadays pose the question: Is Alleman the same kind of man? He too seems to be crazy, even more insane than was Ardial; but maybe this is just because he can't talk. But maybe he can talk. Maybe he has a new language, one that will one day be understood. Maybe some day people will be sorry that they have treated him in the way they do now.

11

Enjoying Life

I N PALAU, as in so many other parts of the "primitive world" visited by outsiders, there has been a clash of philosophies on, among other things, the purpose of work. Whereas the Palauan has traditionally viewed leisure as a natural right interfered with, out of unfortunate necessity, by the requirement of working to sustain it, the Western world has come to look upon it as a reward for work. It has not been easy for the islanders to grasp this notion, or if they understand it, to accept it fully and make of it a guide to action. But the emphasis upon systematized labor, seriousness of purpose, foresight, progress, and other Western values has been so insistent that a significant shift in this direction has taken place. Most enterprising Westerners will say that there is still much room for improvement, but viewing the present from the perspective of the past reveals a major change in the overall pattern of pleasure seeking.

Once there was a much more intimate union of work and play than there is now. Many economic activities, especially those of the men, were by their nature pleasurable. Most men will agree that hunting and fishing are a diversion that can be exciting. For the Palauans, they very evidently have an element of sheer fun. No one can watch a man stalking a pigeon with a blowgun or chasing a fish with a spear without realizing how much enjoyment can be derived from such activities. They are like a game, a contest of wit and skill, the more challenging because the odds are more even with the use of primitive weapons.

Even less thrilling pursuits have their rewards in the satisfaction of their skillful accomplishment. Palauan carpenters, carvers, and other artisans know the pleasure which attends the painstaking labor of the master craftsman, a vanishing pleasure in a machine-made civilization or one in which a work of art must be produced in matched sets for home decoration or in job lots for mass sales and rapid turnovers. To a great extent community service and group effort of all sorts is also painless labor. This is because it is infused with sociability. When people do things together not only because they must be done but because the people like to be together, work is a reason for having a good time; or it may very well be the other way around, for the two aspects of the situation are mutually stimulating. The Palauans still draw heavily upon their tradition of playful work or workful play, though individualism is etching away its foundations. There is a spontaneous interchange of hands in a group of working Palauans that is striking to an observer accustomed to an assembly-line production or even to the job compartmentalization of a construction gang or the single-task intensity of a garment factory. There is, moreover, a gaiety that cannot be missed, much yelling, joking, and gesturing that distracts and cuts into efficiency but keeps people on the job.

One consequence of the increasing separation of fun and work in modern times has been their segregation in time and place. In Palau, every day was the same until the arrival of the missionaries and later the teachers and other government employees. At the present time the weekend holiday begins at noon on Saturday, and no systematic work is done from then on through Sunday. Comparatively few people attend church regularly, but all observe Sunday as a day of rest and recreation. It is the day for getting dressed up and for visiting or idling at home. The Japanese encouraged group sports, especially baseball, and there were leagues with a schedule of games on week-ends. School is in session Monday through Friday and all celebrations con-nected with its activities are reserved for Saturday or Sunday.

The separation of play and work has been accompanied by a curtailment of the former. Mostly this has been a result of the suppression of those aspects of Palauan life that the Germans and their successors could not tol-erate. In some cases there was a direct assault on idleness or frivolity; in others the effect was indirect, the elimination of one institution forcing the abandonment of another. All of the rituals surrounding life crises have been abbreviated or abandoned entirely as superstitious lore and mummery. Funeral and birth rites have lost their pageantry and conviction. They never were fun in the sense of being jubilant occasions; but they did intensify sociability and invite solemn and artistic play with social behavior. With the passing of club life has gone the spirited competition that infused it and the companionship that it provided. This and the elimination of warfare has left a void that has not been filled by substitute forms of excitement to occupy the leisure time of the men.

The squeezing of fun out of the daily round has made what fun there is more artificial. It has become planned pleasure and so has taken on a theatrical character. It is rehearsed and staged, not a spontaneous outgrowth of a situa-tion. Practically all artistic effort is of this character. Where once women made fine mats for the pleasure of exercising their talent and winning the admiration of other skilled artisans, they now make inferior ones for sale to less dis-criminating foreigners. So too with the men's plaques copied or fictionalized from the decorations of the club houses. Whereas they once carved them to fit into the context of Palauan culture, they now make them as curios and exotics in incongruous settings. The same artificiality is evident in the less subtle forms of play. Dancing and singing were once an integral part of living, something that children learned along with other patterns of behavior and that adults were prepared to do when the occasion called for them. Over the years, these occasions have become infrequent, and young people today regard them as outmoded. They tend to regard native-style dancing and singing as quaint, and many do not want to be seen in this light. They have not failed to note that American males, in particular, prefer to be amused by others rather than to participate, except in Western-style dancing and community singing. In any case, native dancing has come to be considered unmasculine and childish.

Loss of spontaneity and naturalness has in modern times been accompanied by a division between spectators and actors. There have always been some Palauans who were better singers and dancers than others, but they were only leaders of the rest, not performers for an audience. Everyone joined in, regardless of his ability, for the enjoyment it gave him. At present there is a tendency for a spectator group to form, leaving the stage to the bolder if not more talented individuals. The folk aspect of celebrations has given way to an active-passive division among the celebrants.

The Palauans have been as receptive to foreign games and sports as to other aspects of culture. To a large extent this receptivity explains the shift in amusement patterns, for with the abandonment of native forms there has been a substitution not only of alien activities but of alien concepts. Although there has been some mingling, more often the new has displaced the old.

School children are enthusiastic contestants. They swarm out of classrooms to play a variety of games during recess. Baseball is most popular and is played the year around. Several games on the order of prisoners' base and keep-away are played with basketballs by boys and girls together. Besides these sports, in which teams are made up spontaneously, athletic contests of several sorts are organized and encouraged by teachers on specific days during the week. Teachers also take their classes on picnics on the beach—a truly American innovation but not very novel, for the Palauans spend much of their time on or near the beach fighting flies and eating sand.

Card games played for money are entertainments of the "fast set"— those who have learned them by watching Japanese and American servicemen. They intersperse Japanese and American calls and counts with Palauan translations. The more sophisticated interject "next time," "sorry boys," and "come again" at any point in the play—meaningless but impressive evidences of inside knowledge. Stakes are 5 or 10 cents, called that or their Palauan or Japanese equivalents.

The Palauans have no musical instruments but they are musical. School children under the instruction of a capable teacher harmonize beautifully with not so much as a pitch pipe to assist them. Eager to please the Americans, they attempt to master the "Star Spangled Banner" and "Swanee River" and put on a gala display for official school visitors. They are as proud of their vocal accomplishments as of their school records.

The most popular dance is one that has been copied from the Trukese workers brought to Angaur in 1917. It gives the greatest freedom to improvisation and individuality; and it is obviously enjoyed for this reason as well as for the vigor of expression that it permits. The dancers, young men or women, or sometimes both, form a line facing the audience and go through an indefinite series of routines, each accompanied by a song separated by intervals when the dancers do nothing but mark time with a shuffling kick. Each time the tramping continues until someone starts a song; while it is going on, the leader, who is in front of the line, calls "one, two, three, four" in Japanese or English, or "left, right"—invariably the reverse of what it should be. When a song and its accompanying dance routine end, the leader calls "march," and the tramping begins. Sometimes the line of dancers calls off, military fashion. The action is lively and loud. It is punctuated by high-pitched wavering yells by anyone feeling the urge. The show ends with the leader calling out "wan-na-stop!" to a three-part step in unison.

The international character of this dance is even more marked in the song and dance routines into which the tramping merges. They are the inventions of participants who teach the rest and lead them during a performance. None is standardized, and ideally none is carried over from one performance to another. They are as varied as Palauan ingenuity can make them, which means that they are new combinations of elements drawn from all kinds of entertainments. Many of the body movements accompanying the songs are combinations of a few basic features—foot tapping, hip slapping, head turning —that could be Trukese or Palauan. The rest are American, Japanese, or Japanese-American in origin, but modified and distorted. There are steps that are said to be from the tango, one-step, two-step, waltz, fox trot, and Charleston; there are stilted posturings and formalized gestures taken from Japanese drama; and there are a great many bits of action that the Japanese thought were American and that the Palauans think are Japanese.

Often the action is an interpretation of the theme of the song sung to accompany it. Original compositions are welcome but they are rare these days. There are Palauan love songs, lullabies, and songs of praise that could be incorporated into the dance, but only the older people know them. The young are the performers and they prefer something exotic even if it is meaningless— a Japanese love song in Yapese, for example. The results can be complex and more amusing than the performers realize. It is genuine entertainment to witness a Palauan imitation of a Japanese imitating an American interpreting "China Town" or "Mexicali Rose."

The movies have had a great effect on these performances as well as on other aspects of Palauan life. The Japanese did not provide theatrical entertainment for the Palauans and, since they did not welcome them in their midst, in effect they withheld their own forms of entertainment from them. Still, there were indoctrinational films, out-of-door shows, and displays which were instructive in one way or another. Now, ever since the arrival of the Americans, there is an open-air theatre in Koror to which Palauans have been admitted, as well as many kinds of films and exhibits in schools and in the Community Center. From commercial films the Palauans get a slanted view of American life out of which they make their own selection of favorite subjects. Most fans like cartoons, westerns, and outdoor sports; adolescents are fascinated by the pomp and glitter of high-society stories which they never completely comprehend even with an explanation. Some of their antics in their own shows are dramatic efforts inspired by these exhibits, mostly grade B and of ancient vintage, and by equally antique musical recordings. It is not surprising, then, to see an act in which girls pair off for an interpretation of the Japanese version of "My Blue Heaven" with naive sentimental postures and facial expressions reminiscent of the dramatics of silent-film days.

The Palauans have taken three dances from the Yapese, two for women and one for men. In one of these, two rows of women are seated back to back with legs drawn up to one side. All of the "dancing" is therefore done with hands, arms, and head. There is an ordered routine of hand claps, arm and thigh slaps, and arm rotations. The most distinctive feature is a delicately synchronized movement of the head and hands: the arms are raised chest high and bent at the elbows, and the hands pivot on the wrists in time with a turning of the head from side to side. The delicate posturing and the undulations of the upper body recall the stylized movements of the Balinese legong. The song for this performance is rapid and lilting. It is used to carry a refrain composed for the occasion to honor a chief.

The men's dance of Yapese origin is also a sitting dance which usually parallels that of the women and sometimes is a parody of it. The other Yapese women's dance is lively and brash. The performers stand in two lines, pivoting and revolving in place while their arms wave and their hips wiggle, hula style. The motion of the hips is suggestive and approaches the erotic, especially when at regular intervals the women bend to a crouch as they loudly clap their hands and their leader sings out impromptu sing-song phrases contrived to evoke laughter: "Come down, come down," "very good, very good," "one, two, three, four," in any one of three or four languages. The Palauans like to entertain the Americans with this dance, for usually before it is over the diversion becomes mutual. In fact, they regularly use it to get spectator participation. Everyone is encouraged to clap hands, and as the excitement develops, young men go into the audience to urge the more exuberant, men or women, to join the dancing line. The dance has no end. It runs to a stop when exhaustion overtakes the performers.

The only Palauan dance that has survived is one performed by older women. For it the women stand in two lines that are divided in half, the two halves facing each other. Each woman holds two wands with streamers attached to one end. The dance is performed on one spot and consists of lifting one heel at a time and then softly lowering it as the other foot is lifted and the body is pivoted through a right angle. The foot movements are synchronized with arm, shoulder, and head movements, and a rolling motion of the hips— again the hula but much subdued. Each phase of the dance lasts about ten minutes and ends with the women tapping their wands and straightening up. The song they sing is slow and mournful. It is solemn, and tells of some historical event being memorialized.

Part of any holiday consists of getting dressed up, and the Palauans do this American style as best they can with their limited means and the help of a mail-order catalogue. Old women are the drabbest dressers. Once they had fancy fiber skirts which they wore with an exaggerated swagger; now they may have a Sunday dress, and if they are rich a relatively inconspicuous piece of Palauan money to tie at their throats. Breech cloths were banned by the Japanese along with grass skirts. So was the fancy male coiffure—long hair swirled into a knot on the left side of the head and held by a slender ornamental comb. Ordinarily men now wear shorts and usually a short-sleeved shirt. On festive occasions they fully cover themselves with long pants, long-sleeved shirts, shoes, and sun helmets. Footwear varies from field shoes to tennis oxfords to rubber boots, depending upon status and pretension. Fit is a secondary consideration in all these items, for it is usually difficult to achieve without an understanding of catalogue sizes. The most important thing is to look like some kind of an American—even if it is uncomfortable. The struggle is evident when Americans are invited to a celebration. With the departure of the guests there is a general shedding of clothes, as there is during the relaxed intervals during a long holiday. Shoes, especially, are commonly carried to and from the fringes of attention.

Young women dress more colorfully and gracefully. Many of them make their own dresses and in these their taste runs to yokes and shoulder frills and ruffles. An all-white ensemble of white shoes, socks, and dress is considered the most stylish, but white blouses and jackets slipped over a colored dress are almost as appealing. Long ear pendants of gold plate, or less, and ornamental combs are brought out only for real holidays. So are the colored streamers fastened in rosettes on the chest like a delegate's badge. Handkerchiefs are daintily tucked in jacket pockets or folded over belts at one hip. Lipstick and rouge have become fairly common. Face powder often has an arresting effect and it is something that not everybody can manage. High-heeled shoes are also in this category. Boys as well as girls have a penchant for colored glasses for both day and evening wear.

Many Palauans have dramatic talent which they have learned to exercise in skits which they call *shibais* in imitation of the Japanese. Both men and women present them, but not as a mixed company. They are pantomimes accompanied by songs and exaggerated posturings, and the ubiquitous hip wiggle is somehow worked into the action of the plot. All are funny, some slapstick. Most are satires lampooning some individual or ridiculing an idea or a custom. The parts are worked out and rehearsed, but there is a great deal of spontaneity on stage. The actors use a minimum of accessories and much is left to the imagination of the audience. There are sporadic and fleeting suggestions of character representation in the facial make-up, but mostly this is fanciful and weird, applied for humorous effect. The costuming is more associated with character and situational portrayal but it is still exaggerated and grotesque. In-character dress is less valued than oddity of fit or combination. Actors portraying Palauan men wear shorts with loin cloths pulled over them; men playing the part of women exaggerate sexual characteristics; those cast as Japanese soldiers wear every available kind and combination of uniform including the American—their swords are wood saws, their guns are blowguns.

While the United States Navy was still in control of the islands, one of the northern districts held a big celebration, a *kledol,* honoring another district which had helped it rehabilitate itself. Part of the festivities included the presentation of many dances of the kind described above and a number of *shibais.* The idea throughout was to make spectators laugh; and while the substance of the *shibais* were matters of very serious concern to some people, the humorous aspects of each situation were highlighted and emphasized.

One of the skits portrayed a canoe load of Yapese men—of whose intelligence the Palauans have a low opinion—attacking a battleship. The warriors wore a few leaves on a band around their waists, symbolic of the grass skirts of Yapese women. They carried sticks for spears and wielded coconut fronds for paddles. The hip wiggling was synchronized with the rowing action. The battleship was represented by a man in a soldier's helmet using a spy glass. After much maneuvering and shouting and spear hurling, there was a loud crash backstage and the scene dissolved in confusion and grotesque "dying."

There was another caricature, this time of Okinawans, who are also held in low esteem by most Palauans. Its central character was an improvident husband who was supposed to be seeking employment to support his wife and child but spent his time in strolling around smoking. His wife took in washing; their baby died; they buried it. The male part was taken by a girl wearing shorts pulled over her dress. The action took place as she sang a sentimental song, broken frequently by hip-wiggling exhibitions by both characters.

An episode in the life of a peeping tom brought the most raucous laughter. The girl's part was played by a boy with a cloth over his head and a padded blouse. She entered and slowly crossed the stage, singing a song with many pauses, as she carried her washing to the bathing pool. She was followed by a man hiding behind a few leaves held before his face. At the pool she gave herself and her clothes a thorough washing, wiggling all the while. Finally she detected the man in hiding, screamed and ran for a policeman. The culprit was taken before an American police sergeant. What followed was an uproarious exhibition of American law in action as seen by the Palauans. The few words of English the stern-faced sergeant knew emerged from an otherwise unintelligible mumble with peremptory gestures. There was much confusion on the part of the court, the policeman, the girl, and the accused; but ultimately the case was settled with a conviction and a 10-year jail sentence.

There is no question that the Palauans enjoy watching dances and shows like those given at this three-day *kledol.* But the actors and the hosts complain that the cost and the effort required to stage such a celebration is excessive. There was a great deal of muttering about this one. One day or evening might have been all right, they said, but more than that keeps people from work and is too expensive. The cost of the *kledol* was reckoned by the complainants to be $560, in return for which the visitors gave them six cases of canned rations and $100. Besides, the dancers had practiced nightly, sometimes till dawn, for fifteen days prior to the celebration. This made work out of play.

12

Worshiping Gods

BEFORE THE COMING of the Europeans, the Palauans believed in two main categories of supernatural beings: the spirits of the dead and the beings that may be called gods. Spirits of the dead fell into two groups: the spirits of one's own ancestors and the spirits of the dead of other families or clans. These were called, respectively, *bladek* and *delep*. The former were not feared; rather, they were interviewed, propitiated, and appealed to for help. The *delep*, on the other hand, were more like our conception of ghosts. In general, they were feared, and contact with them in any way was avoided because they were the ancestral dead of other clans, sometimes of distant and unknown clans; and since they were strange, they were likely to be harmful. The spirits of one's own dead ancestors could also be harmful, but they could be supplicated and their anger abated. They would yield to pleas and sacrifices by their living descendants, even though it was believed that they were fickle, jealous, and vindictive at times.

The head of the clan, who bore the family title and was normally the oldest member of his group, acted as a priest in making all formal contacts with its ancestral spirits. He resided in the large house that was the traditional homesite of the clan and he acted for all members of that household as well as for dependents who might be living in other houses. He made offerings to the ancestral spirits in a special part of his house, the left end as one enters the building. This was done when someone fell ill and it was determined that the sickness was caused by the displeasure of a spirit. Spirits were also summoned if the family members wished to converse with them; it was sometimes desirable to get an expression of their wishes with regard to the disposal of some property, or to find out why they had manifested themselves in a certain way. At other times the head of the household, acting in his capacity as clan head, wanted to get the advice and support of his ancestors in some action that he was contemplating in the family interest.

The category of gods was linked with that of ancestral spirits, but the

79

two groups were distinct. Every clan worshipped a god and a goddess who carried titles that were the counterparts of the titles of the men and women who were the leaders of the clan. They had proper names in addition to these titles, just as human beings did. The gods were appealed to in all situations that were deemed to be outside the sphere of activity of the ancestral spirits; and they, because they had always been gods and never men, were considered to be more powerful.

Each clan had its own totems with associated food taboos. Some plant or animal was forbidden as food to all members of the clan, and they even avoided any direct contact with it. It was thought that the clan gods, and perhaps the spirits of ancestors, quickly punished taboo violations. A person who was foolish enough to ignore them was inflicted with a swelling of the stomach or by some other ailment which could be relieved only by making an offering.

While clan dieties were of primary importance to members of their matrilineal families, some of them had a much wider influence and became the concern of other clans as well. In fact, the gods were graded in importance along with the families of their descendants. The gods of the ranking clan in a village were conceived to be more potent than the gods of the other clans, and they could exercise controls in both the supernatural world and in the earthly sphere just as their living descendants manipulated the controls in the village. The importance of the god of the pre-eminent clan was so great that its totemic taboos were added to those of every other clan, thus making them village-wide in application.

A child could not kill or eat the totem of either parent. The prohibition was passed on to the next generation, and therefore a child recognized the taboos of his four grandparents. With time, the requirement was relaxed in the male but not the female line. Thus, a person continued to observe a taboo that was transmitted matrilineally, but did not observe any on his father's side beyond those of his grandfather.

Each clan had a shrine in the yard of its homesite erected to honor its god. These shrines were of the same general design as the club houses, but were square. They were small, measuring only two or three feet on a side, and were raised on posts. Like the club houses, they were decorated with low relief carvings and paintings. Offerings were placed inside them; hence they were called the handbags of the gods.

The shrine of the village god, who was the tutelary divinity of the ranking family, was larger than the rest and was more elaborately decorated. It occupied the place of honor, in the approximate center of the village, adjacent to the chiefs' club houses. Offerings were made there when any undertaking of community concern was launched, such as a war, or a celebration in honor of visitors from other districts.

Certain gods were known and worshipped in several districts, and perhaps over a good part of the islands. They were superior to district deities, and there is a mythology about them which testifies to their greater importance; some are regarded as elemental or primary gods and goddesses from which the others derived. It is possible that they were at one time simply the spirits of certain clans which in time became influential politically.

A *korong* was another intermediary between gods and men who functioned in a different capacity from that of the clan or household priest. The position was not inheritable, for a *korong* might be anyone who had received the call to become a medium for the expression of a god's wishes. He manifested tendencies to fulfill his role as a medium by his strange behavior; often, for example, he was seized with fits of yawning or coughing. No attention was paid to his aberrations unless he showed some supernatural sign of his calling. When he insisted upon going through the village shouting that he was a god and behaving in ways he thought the god should behave, people began to take notice and consider seriously whether there might not be some truth in what he said.

A *korong* was not simply the delegate of the god who had chosen him as a medium; he *was* that god upon those occasions when he functioned in his official capacity. It was believed that the god took possession of his body and spoke through his mouth, and at such times he was no longer a human being. The possession of his body was manifested in various ways, depending upon the nature of the god. In almost all cases the onset of his seizure was marked by violent tremors. Thereafter he might continue to tremble or go into a trance. What he said was taken to be the words of the god, and he pretended not to know what he had said when he gained control of himself.

Such a man was always an important person in his village, and sometimes his reputation extended far beyond. In some places the *korong* of the principal god held a position that was at least equivalent to that of the first chief. Because it often happened that he was by birth a low-class person, there can be no doubt that the chiefs had considerable discretion in according him the recognition of being the medium of an important god.

In addition to being politically powerful, *korongs* also became wealthy. Unlike chiefs, wealth came to them not from inheritance but from payment for services. Offerings that were made to their gods were kept by them. Food was always acceptable, as was betel, but money was also offered. Gods were summoned to sanction any group undertaking, and also to cause and cure illnesses. For some illnesses, as diagnosed by a *korong,* an offering in the form of a pig or some other valuable food item had to be prepared by the relatives of the sick person to feed an angry spirit. At other times it was said that a person became ill because of some offense that he or some relative of his had committed against another person. In this case a payment of money, food, or other goods had to be tendered to the offended individual in order to appease the wrath of his ancestral spirit. Sometimes a person was quite unaware of wrongdoing. At times it was said that the spirit of a sick man's ancestor had offended the ancestor of another living man. Both men were, of course, ignorant of this and learned of it only through a *korong.* The *korong* told his patient the name of the living descendant of the offended spirit to whom the property payments had to be made in order that he might be cured.

There was a variety of religious specialists who knew the proper ritual for specific occasions. In fact, all professionals were in possession of certain mystic lore that was essential to their work. Canoe makers and house builders had to know the incantations requisite for their trade; the same was true for professional mid-wives, warriors, and expert fishermen. Some individuals were especially qualified to cast love spells for a price; another class of diviners was appealed to on any occasion about which there was some anxiety. Divination took many forms, among them the observation of cloud formations, the flight of birds, the ragged edges of certain broken objects, and the casting of counters whose fall in a certain pattern gave the answers to questions about the future. Finally, there was a category of religious specialists properly called magicians. For a price, they used their knowledge to cast spells upon the enemies of their clients or employed counter-magic to break the spell of other magicians. Contagious magic seems to have been most popular. With this a magician effected his purpose through the use of some object that had been in intimate association with his victim, such as an article of his clothing, a hair, or, most frequently, his cast-off betel quid.

For the most part, Palauan religion no longer exists. There is not much reason to suppose that the beliefs that have persisted exist as an integrated system in the minds of those who remember them. A still lesser degree of integration exists in the practices which have survived. The young people, those who have been educated under the Japanese, cling to superstitions deriving from the old system; they have fears and personal avoidances but they do not attach them to any system of belief. Much the same can be said of the older people, except that they understand the background of their fears and observances somewhat better. Nativistic forms at times obtrude from an uncertain state of mind or show themselves through a thin covering of Christianity.

The first Christian missionaries in the Palauas were Capuchins. They arrived in Koror in 1866, and a short time later established stations on Babeldaob. One of these missions was in Alap, and its success, and seemingly that of others under the Spanish Catholics, was not encouraging. The priest stayed only a few years at Alap, although he and his co-workers did break the ground for their successors. They introduced the Palauans to Christian ideology and familiarized them with the Spanish words *dios* and *diablo,* which are still employed, even by other missionaries. They also printed catechisms in the vernacular, some of which are still in the possession of Palauan Catholics.

The first Protestant missionary, a German, arrived in Koror in 1930. He was joined by a colleague in 1932. Both of these men worked actively on Babeldaob, establishing missions and lay preaching units in several districts. Later, missionaries of other sects, among them the Seventh Day Adventists, were encouraged by the Japanese.

Protestant church services follow a regular order in the villages. They begin with a hymn, the words of which, if necessary, can be found in the small pamphlet which most members have. The leader then offers a prayer, which is followed by a hymn and an antiphonal reading from the catechism with responses from the congregation. Again there is a hymn, after which the leader reads a text and then delivers a sermon which lasts for 15 or 20 minutes. Another hymn follows, and the service concludes with everyone reciting the Lord's Prayer and singing a final hymn.

As so frequently is the case on the frontiers of Christianity, Palau has had its native religious leaders who claim to have had a divine revelation announcing a new era. Temudad, the founder of the *Modekne* cult, was such a man. He was a policeman under the German regime, during which time he worked on Angaur. Some members of the cult say that as a youth he was mischievous and bad, "running after girls and stealing." Apparently, at the time of his close association with the Germans he received some religious instruction and reformed. It is said that he learned to read and write, and that he came into possession of some religious book which he studied. During these years, he was a vigorous man with a good presence and a persuasive manner of speaking.

When his work on Angaur was finished, he returned to his home village. Not many years later he became seriously ill, was confined to his bed, and was expected to die. His sickness seemed to affect his mind, for he became "silly." He was sick for about a year, during which time he began to act like a *korong*. He wrapped a red cloth about his head and went around the village shouting that he was a certain god. He spoke in the first person in the voice of the god that he supposed was possessing him. At the same time he began to accuse people of committing various sins. He would approach a man and tell him that he had stolen something, or that he had damaged someone's property, or that he had injured someone, or that he had committed adultery. At first no one paid any attention to him, or tried not to. The climax in his gradual acceptance as a man possessing divine revelation came when he allegedly raised a child from the dead.

Temudad denounced the sins of adultery, lying, stealing, and murder. He prohibited drinking, smoking, and betel chewing. He declared the equality of all men before god, and he seems to have extended this doctrine into the temporal field, for it is said of him—by his admirers at least—that he deplored the system which permits the rich to get richer at the expense of the poor. He exhorted his followers to abandon several of their old customs. He censured magicians and *korongs* for their pretensions, but especially for extorting money from their clients. He said that *korongs* who levied a payment of food on a sick person, so that gods could appease their hunger, were hypocrites because their gods were false; true gods cannot consume food. His most striking and well-remembered innovation was the condemnation of the food taboos of the totem plants and animals. He said that they were foolish because the true god made foods to be used by all his people and no one should be denied any of them.

The rituals of the *Modekne* cult are confined to meetings similar to the services of Christian congregations, and to healing ceremonies, with an emphasis upon the latter. All sins are believed to cause illness. Several cures are possible, however. Considerable use was made by Temudad of a purification water, a decoction of boiled leaves. Patients were either bathed in this or were advised to drink it. Sometimes either this or blessed water was used to sprinkle on a sick person. For some types of illnesses it was necessary to exorcise evil spirits that had taken possession of the patient's body. In such cases the person was massaged, or a cloth with a cross on it was used to flick or brush the spirit away from his body and out of the house. For relief of some ills, Temudad reverted to the old custom of requiring a payment of money by the patient to someone who had been injured or offended by him.

After Temudad's death, in 1928, the beliefs and practices of the cult took a reactionary turn. He had been progressive in the sense that he either consciously or unconsciously adopted many Christian principles and was not averse to accepting other cultural innovations; nor was he outwardly opposed to foreign control. His successor was Ongesi, and under his influence the cult embraced several nativistic elements. Foreign songs were banned. Only Palauan foods were acceptable to members, and the food had to be served in native dishes. Crockery and metal pots and pans were forbidden. Ongesi preached that the dark-skinned Palauans were a different kind of men from the light-skinned peoples and that their destinies must be different. He said that the white men, including the Japanese, walked along one road while the Palauans walked along another, and the two ways could never meet. Consequently, there were two heavens, one for the Palauans and another for foreigners.

The Japanese began to take action against the cult's leaders while Temudad was still alive. They became alarmed because of its popularity and because they sensed something subversive in its appeals to native tradition. While the antiforeign elements in the cult doctrine were the most objectionable aspects for the Japanese, they drew up a list of complaints on ethical and other grounds. They charged its leaders with being false prophets and with robbing the people under false pretenses. They said that the cult was demoralizing; that it caused people to waste their time away from productive labor and thereby impoverished them. They were opposed to its healing practices which were unscientific and in many cases unhygienic, as for example when its followers drank various kinds of filthy liquids. They appear to have been alarmed also over the widely circulated and exaggerated reports crediting Temudad with unlimited powers of resurrecting the dead.

Temudad was imprisoned and died in jail. According to legend, he knew when he was going to die and predicted the time to the hour. Ongesi was imprisoned on Saipan during World War II and at its conclusion was released by the Americans. One day he attacked another man and seriously injured him. His victim was taken to the hospital and finally recovered, but in the meantime Ongesi hanged himself.

American authorities have prohibited *Modekne* adherents from practicing faith healing and other unscientific means of curing injuries and sicknesses. Since this element has become the core of cult activities and the principal interest of its members, the prohibition has amounted to a virtual ban on the cult itself—at least, those who belong to it make this interpretation. They believe that their activities are outlawed and therefore they conceal them. They have been told that they worship the devil, but they deny this, saying that they fight evil spirits and that Temudad himself drove the devil out of the islands. They maintain that they are the most upright of the Palauans because they refuse to break the law, not because it is a law, but because they have moral scruples against violating it. They say that they must follow the teachings of their leaders because it is true that there is one road for black men and another for white men and the two can never meet.

13

Palauan Journal

Editorial Introduction

Anthropologists often speak of the desirability of keeping a diary for each day in the field. Many do, but few publish them. Homer Barnett's selections from his own journal, kept while he was doing fieldwork on Palau, are of particular value. They not only show the nature of such a diary, but also illustrate the events that make up fieldwork from day to day.

His journal illustrates that much fieldwork consists of waiting for things to happen, being friendly, receptive, and present. The approach is low key, and nonthreatening. The role of the participant observer becomes clear. He is something more than an honored guest and something less than one of the people. It is clear that he is able to see what is going on because he is present, though not always really participating as a full member of the group. Even in the intimacy of his relationship with the people there is some distance between him and his informants. This is always true, but here in this journal we can see the nature of this distance clearly. To be invited to all the places he went and to all of the affairs he participated in as guest, he had to be attractive, trusted, and available. This does not make Homer Barnett a Palauan.

But at the same time he was accepted as an elder brother by one of his closest assistants. This relationship was of great significance. Homer Barnett was, therefore, inside and outside the Palauan system simultaneously. This is usually the anthropologist's position. "Palauan Journal" makes this clear.

Homer Barnett was born in Bisbee, Arizona. He began his anthropological career with archeological fieldwork near Taft, California, in 1932. In

Homer Barnett and Azu.

1934 and again during 1935–1936 he did fieldwork among Indian tribes, first in southwestern Oregon and then among the Salish of British Columbia. Later he did fieldwork among the Klamath, Yurok, the Tsimshian, and the Yakima, all Northwest Coast people. He has long had a special interest in the Pacific Islands. In 1947–1948 he lived in a Palauan village, in 1952–1953 he visited Fiji and New Caledonia, in 1955 Netherlands New Guinea, in 1961 Australian New Guinea, in 1962 the Solomon Islands, and in 1966–1968 Australia. As Staff Anthropologist for the U.S. Government's Trust Territory of the Pacific Islands, he visited all the major island groups of American Micronesia with extended revisits to Palau to deal with special problems arising from Palauan adaptations to changing conditions. He has also been an adviser to the Netherlands New Guinea government on its native welfare programs and a member of the Research Council of the South Pacific Commission, a body of social scientists that recommends studies of native and administrative needs as traditional patterns are modified through contact with alien cultures and demands. He is a Professor of Anthropology at the University of Oregon where he has taught since 1939. In 1961 he was President of the Society for Applied Anthropology. He has written many articles on cultural process and is particularly well known for his book, *Innovation: the Basis of Cultural Change*, first published in 1953. His books also include *Palauan Society, Anthropology in Administration, Indian Shakers,* and *The Coast Salish of British Columbia.*

He explains how he came into anthropology:

I wandered into anthropology at the University of California in Berkeley as a graduate student. My undergraduate years were spent at Stanford, where no course on the subject was given at the time. I knew what I wanted to do and be, but I didn't know the name of it. I knew that I wanted to understand people, all people, because I came from a part of the country where race prejudice was rampant and at times violent. The closest I could get to this at Stanford was in philosophy and in courses on Russian and Chinese literature. Then, after five years of knocking around the world as a seaman on various freighters, I reluctantly decided to become a teacher, a high school teacher. That was in 1932 when the economic bottom had fallen out of everything and I came to the happy conclusion that I would rather starve as a student than as an unsuccessful salesman of subscriptions to the *San Francisco Chronicle*. During a semester of boredom in the curriculum for teacher aspirants at the University of California, I combed through the catalogue of courses and made up my mind to go all the way and try one called "Primitive Society." That did it. From then on anthropology has been not only my vocation but my avocation. I feel myself lucky in that I cannot and do not want to distinguish between the two. I have been playing at my work and working at my play ever since.

G. D. S.

Preface

From August 23, 1947 until May 21, 1948 Allan Murphy, a graduate student, hereafter usually referred to as Al, and I lived in a small village in the northern part of the Palau Islands. At that time the U.S. Navy administered the islands under a civilian code of law. Ulimang, the hamlet in which we lived, was one of five in the district of Ngarard, the others being Ahol, Ngbuked, Alap, and Geklau.

Our basic problem was to learn the Palauan language. Charlie Simmons was the only Palauan—his father was German—who could speak English, and he was in the employ of the administration at the capital in Koror as an interpreter and factotum. He was loaned to us for the first week of our residence in Ulimang. Beyond that assistance, we had only a minimal English-Palauan word and phrase list; no grammar of the language.

The narrative that follows consists of excerpts from the journal that I kept. The entries relate my day-by-day experiences and reactions to life in Ulimang. Necessarily they are much condensed. In addition to the journal, I recorded

Azu's father.

Lagoon near Ulimang.

detailed ethnographic data in notebooks. In the interests of conserving space
and the reader's patience, the entire record of some days and cross references to
my notebooks have been deleted. In several places I have entered parenthetic
statements to inform the reader about omitted data relevant to the subject
matter included. The names of persons have been altered. Other than these
changes, the excerpts are printed as they were written. Let the prepositions fall
where they may.

August 23   We were taken from Koror to Ngarard by two Navy vessels. We
landed somewhat upriver at a house in the hamlet of Ngbuked. Our interpreter,
Charlie Simmons, told us to remain in the boat until the chief of Ngbuked was
summoned. When he arrived we shook hands and, after some conversation
between him and Charlie, we went ashore. The young men who were to carry
our heavy gear were fishing, so it was decided that the chief, Charlie, Al, and I
should go on to Ulimang and send men for our equipment later. We ascended
a low central crest along a wide, cleared pathway through Ngbuked, the chief
of the village in the lead. Houses, some of them of the old-type construction,
were irregularly spaced off the pathway that over most of its length through the
hamlet was paved with stones. On the top of the rise was a men's clubhouse, in
about the center of the hamlet. At one end there was a siren. Charlie sounded

it three times—the call for an assembly of the people of Ulimang, of which Charlie is a chief.

After about twenty-five minutes we arrived at Ulimang, on the east coast. A middle-aged man came to meet us. We sat on a high bench on the edge of the school grounds while he sat on the ground in front of us. After a short talk we proceeded to the schoolhouse where we were to stay until other arrangements could be made. On the way to Ulimang a few women in doorways spoke to the two chiefs as we passed, but I was impressed by the apparent lack of curiosity about us. Even the children seemed indifferent. Heads were not hanging out of doorways; none apparently appeared from cover. People did not follow or congregate around us. There were several children playing on the broad sandy schoolyard, but they remained where they were, and only came near some time after we had stopped and two more chiefs from nearby villages arrived to greet us.

For the rest of the afternoon, until about 4:30, we sat with the chiefs while they chatted. In the meantime, school boys and girls were sent to get such pieces of our equipment as they could carry. By 5:00 I was getting rather hungry, and was undecided as to what to do. Finally Charlie explained that the first chief of the district, whom we had met in Koror, had sent a message saying that we were to arrive on the following day, and that the people had intended getting a feast ready for us then. As it was, food was being prepared but it would be late in coming. It did arrive after dark, brought by two women on trays carried on their heads. The school teacher had lighted a lamp on our table in the school-

Author's house in Palau.

room building. He helped set the food before us. We ate alone while the Palauans sat outside talking. After we had eaten we joined them. Charlie asked whether we wanted food brought to us each day, or whether we wanted a girl or a boy assigned to help us prepare our food. I explained that we would do our own cooking and most of our other domestic chores.

Before eating we went to see a house nearby. It was being built by a young man, Kai by name, for his own use, but it was offered to us. It was quite suitable and I was pleased at our good luck, but I tried to make it plain to Charlie that we did not want to take it at the inconvenience of the owner. I was assured that he had enough room in another house just back of the one that we would occupy,

Old-type house.

which did not convince me, and I was determined to compensate him in some way.

August 24 The canned foods that we have brought with us are mostly the so-called C rations issued by the military government for its personnel. They are, I trust, nutritious, but they are nonetheless tasteless. I have realized over the past month in passing through Guam and Koror that one of my personal needs is for American-style fresh vegetables—carrots and cabbage exempted. I could add fresh beef, but that is out of reason, because here there is only fish, which I must learn to like. I think I will start a vegetable garden. If it succeeds that would amaze no one more than myself.

August 27 No progress has been made toward getting settled in our house. Monday afternoon Charlie told us we could move in yesterday. We got packed in the morning, but no one came for our baggage, and since we are regarded as chiefs it would be beneath their expectations of us to transport our own effects. This attitude has its advantages but it belongs to another situation. If the people continue to regard us as sahibs the social distance thereby created will deny us the participation that is essential to our purposes. I am referred to and addressed as "Doctor," which may set up still another barrier. This stems from the auspices of the military government, from which I want to disassociate myself as much as possible. Charlie told me earlier that the Ulimang people were notified in advance by the officials in Koror that a "Doctor Somebody" would be coming to live in their village.

Yesterday I gave a package of mints to the oldest girl among about twenty children playing on the schoolground. The rest displayed no eagerness or curiosity about it, even the smallest of them, aged three to five years. The girl to whom I gave the mints walked around with them for awhile and all the children continued to play as they had done before. Finally, after fifteen or twenty minutes they all sat in the shade and the girl proceeded to divide the candy among them, the others sitting in a ring about her. I gave the same girl a package of mints today under the same conditions, and the same thing happened. The children, all of whom seem to be residents of this village, play most of the day on the schoolgrounds. They pay no attention to us, and remain at the opposite corner from us. This is presumably their normal habit. However, I am beginning to suspect that they, as well as the adults of this village, have been told to ignore us, or at least not to bother us.

August 28 One of the school teachers came to ask for help with his English, beginning tomorrow night. I welcomed this as I have hoped to get as much from the teachers as I know they are hoping to get from us. This particular teacher, Pelew, is eager to learn English, not only for the advantage it will give him in dealing with Americans, but because he must teach his pupils how to read, write, and speak it. His command of it now is minimal. He knows the Japanese language—which was the one used in the schools that he attended before the Americans arrived—and he owns a Japanese-English dictionary. Using that he has taught himself about all he knows of English. Working with him, and using that dictionary, I hope to build my Palauan vocabulary.

This afternoon Charlie suggested that we visit Ngbuked and Alap, partly to show us around, and partly because the second chief of Ngarard, who lives in Alap, wanted to give us some oranges in response, I suppose, to the gift of the six cigars which I sent to him yesterday.

August 29 We moved into our house today. On the way we met a rather small young man wearing blue trunks, shoes, and a junior navy officer's cap. His dress was altogether strange by comparison with the other people we have met. In a rather authoritative tone he asked the others if the stuff that they were carrying was ours. The boy who was pushing the cart with some baggage in it said yes and made a gesture offering him the job. All laughed except him. He refused and looked rather angrily at me when I smiled. I was afraid I had made a mistake until one of the men said, "He a little crazy." I kept my eye on him until we got into the house.

Charlie and two other chiefs were already there sitting on our kitchen floor when we arrived. The young men who had helped with the moving sat in what was to be our dining room, while the "Crazy One" joined us in the kitchen. Throughout the time he was present he identified himself with the chiefs, and even overreached them. He made free with the second chief's betel, despite the latter's unobtrusive and fatherly objection. I laid two cartons of cigarettes and about a dozen spools of colored thread on the floor and told Charlie they were for the men and women who had made the house ready for us earlier during the week. Then I set out another and indicated that a package should go to each one for this morning's work. The chiefs proceeded to enumerate the individual men who had helped, and laid out packages of cigarettes by villages. The "Crazy One" took a bold part in this distribution, passing the cigarettes to those who were to get them and repeating the words of the chiefs. Once or twice a remark was made to him by one of the three chiefs, and the other men smiled or laughed. Finally, the second chief told the young men to go, and had to request and repeat his request directly but quietly for the "Crazy One" to leave also.

August 30   We continued intermittently with our household chores through the day. Time goes fast and we seem to accomplish very little, the principal reason being that someone drops by, we invite him in, give him cigarettes, and try to extend our vocabulary and improve our pronunciation. Naturally this is time-consuming. We are anxious also to build goodwill and to be accepted casually. We want the people to come to us rather than the other way around until later on.

September 2   Yesterday was the first day of school. Today as I passed the schoolground where the children were playing, those who are from other villages and who had not yet been near me stood up, faced me, stiffened their arms at their sides, bowed, and said, "Good morning, Sir." Upon our first acquaintance, chiefs have also bowed slightly to me. They have also raised their right hand in salutation. They have ceased to do this, or do it only hesitantly, apparently in response to my rather offhand, inconsistent attention to it myself. I notice that the children in this village have ceased to raise their hands to me and also to come to attention upon meeting me. I believe that if I had demanded it by my attitude, they would have continued the formality. We are certainly no longer lacking in attention by the children nor the adults. Practically everyone who passes our house—and there are many, for we are on the common path leading from the village center to the bathing and watering place—peers in as he passes by. Sometimes a whole group will do the same. We have practically no privacy, and there are scarcely fifteen minutes when someone is not trying to get a glimpse of us.

None of the teachers can speak even fair English, and they do not know many basic words such as "learn," "means," and the like. I have tried to use charades, my limited Palauan, their limited English, and several Japanese-English dictionaries and phrase books to explain and to be explained to by them. It is on occasions such as these that one is impressed with the really fundamental character of "the meaning of meaning." You soon reach the point beyond which explaining seems impossible.

September 4 I have scarcely moved from the house for two days. Pelew has been here for the past two nights and we have stayed up until 12:00 working on English and Palauan. People continued to bring us bits of food. Kai brought us a fish last night. Pelew had already given us one. Masas, one of the older school boys, brought us two eggs tonight. It has been mainly these three who have brought us food, perhaps because we are neighbors. As yet I do not even know who lives at the other end of the village, because I have been so occupied with those who live near us.

September 7 This afternoon the second chief came to see me bearing gifts— three oranges, three fish, and a chicken. The chicken is so skinny it would be pointless to eat it now, so I set to work to pen it up and feed it for awhile. The chief is jolly, and made a joke which I took to mean that if I used the chicken as a lure others would be drawn to it and I would thereby have a flock. He talked on and I nodded, only partly guessing what he was saying, but I gathered that he wanted to tell me that he would have a carpenter here to build our outhouse—a little matter that has concerned me for some time.

September 8 Al and I hoed the weeds out of a patch of ground in the backyard of our house—the beginning of a garden. Both activities, the outhouse building and the hoeing, were regarded rather humorously by many passers-by. They think, I believe, that trying to raise a garden in our backyard is a silly business of white men. And our pale skin, our larvae-like appearance in shorts probably adds to their amusement. Our chicken has been a source of curiosity for the children and the quiet amusement of several adults. I have penned it in a screened enclosure under the house. Both the pen and the use of the space under the floor is strange to the people. Native chickens run free, and no use at all is made of the area under the elevated floor of the house.

September 9 About 4:30 this afternoon a young man came to ask whether I had a "picture engine." I guessed he meant a camera. And so he did, because he wanted me to take a picture of himself and of Kai's wife and their baby. I was happy to have our cameras introduced in this way; that is, by request. We had not so far brought them out. I took the picture, then suggested one of Kai, then one of the whole family in front of their house.

September 11 There was considerable activity all day. I set our motion picture camera at our front window about noontime, focused it on the section of the path in front of our door, and took a strip of pictures of every passer-by until 4:00 P.M.

September 12 Kai appeared about 3:00 P.M., eager to teach us Palauan. He is very bright and helpful. He stayed until 6:00; then was back again at 8:00. About 9:00 Masas and one of his young friends came by as they have been doing, and we did some more language study to mutual advantage. We got to bed at 11:30, which has come to be normal.

September 16 This has been a very full day, so much so that I have had little time to myself. The Ngbuked chief came as we were washing breakfast dishes around 9:00. He brought a stalk of bananas and three small chickens. I gave him three cigars and a package of cigarettes. He stayed for a full two hours, sitting on the kitchen floor with us. I brought out the recording machine and the motion picture camera for the first time. He asked about the generator that we have not uncrated and that everybody has supposed is for a lighting plant. Actually it is to generate electricity for our steel wire recorder. He wanted to know whether I am Catholic or Protestant and when I replied Protestant he was jubilant—and seemed distressed and puzzled when I added that Murphy is a Catholic. I gathered that he could not understand our living together. Anyway, he invited me to church services in Ngbuked Sunday after next and asked me to bring the camera.

September 17 Isuwut came early and worked all day on our generator. He was able to get it started, but it was difficult. I have my doubts, as I always have had, about its utility. I tried to give Isuwut 50 cents, but he refused. We also asked him in to have lunch but he refused. I urged him, but he said he was not hungry. Apparently none of them will eat with us. Even Charlie, who is otherwise accustomed to associating with Germans, Japanese, and Americans, has been reluctant to do so when other Palauans are present.

September 25 I visited the school today. I went there to set my watch by the school clock, but found that it is set by the sun. I sat in the sixth grade class. They were trying to write English sentences, using "house" and "see" and were having a difficult time. The pupils rise when the teacher enters the room, but otherwise the proceedings are quite informal, though the teacher's attitude is stern and abrupt. The teacher had his class sing for me. The song was the *Star-Spangled Banner*—I think!

October 9 It rained rather hard for an hour again this morning. Yesterday afternoon I decided to transplant some of my house-raised tomato plants, and to set out two or three dozen onions. Our corn has survived—it is 8 or 9 inches high. The pole beans are higher. Melons and squash are doing well. No lettuce has ever showed above ground. Thin hairlike blades of onions have appeared but have died, probably due to lack of water. Three radishes have survived.

October 10 The Ngbuked chief invited me to join the Protestants for the opening of a new church building in Ngerchelong, which is about two and one half hours' walk from here. I declined because I do not want to become closely identified with that or any other element in the community.

October 12 Kai took us out to the reef this morning at low tide. Since it is Sunday and his coconut oil plant was not operating, he was agreeable to the suggestion of our taking pictures of him spearfishing. He was in fact a willing and enthusiastic actor before the movie camera.

October 20 We spent most of the day getting our gasoline engine and our recording machine in operation. We have it set up about 50 yards from the house. By the time the operation was completed we had an interested and a dumbfounded audience, which had collected to observe the activity. We picked up their conversation and played it back to them. For the first time they got the idea, and then Kai explained it all. At the end a small boy wanted to sing a song and did. I asked that the school children come to our house to have their songs recorded.

October 22 The recording experiment with the school children was an unhappy failure. The gasoline engine seemed to run well enough, but there was a pulsation in the current. The songs were badly distorted, due in part to the rise and fall of current intensity—like a lopsided phonograph record. After several attempts to adjust the machine we abandoned the experiment and, much to my disappointment and embarrassment, sent the children back to school.

October 23 We spent the whole morning repairing an air rifle belonging to an old man of Alap. We had previously fixed his flashlight and given him batteries for it. Other people seem to regard our association with him as a little ridiculous. Kai refers to him to me as "Mr. Murphy's Friend" and laughs. The old fellow, whose name is Ackul, has no social position and does not seem to fit well with his society. He repeatedly says that Palau is bad, and that he admires Americans.

October 24 I spent two hours this morning with Pelew at school. He suggested this the night before and I was happy for the chance. This should dispense with so much night study and also keep me in touch with what is going on at the school.

October 25 We set out for Ngbuked about 10:00 A.M. On the way we stopped at Kai's coconut oil plant where all of his helpers (five of them) were sitting around discussing financial matters. We spent a couple of hours talking with them since they had nothing better to do it seemed. Their supply of coconuts was exhausted, and since it was Saturday they were quitting work at noon anyway. We had a very profitable language lesson.

November 2 We returned from our monthly trip to Koror for supplies last night. While there, I borrowed a combination Palauan-German and German-Palauan dictionary from the Protestant missionary. He loaned us a New Testament so we can collate the Palauan translation of St. Luke. He also gave us some printed Sunday school lessons in Palauan. These are very helpful.

November 7 The work on the new office buildings continued today. The older men set up the foundation posts for the new store also. The work proceeded very leisurely. At any one time about half of the men were sitting around talking among themselves and heckling the others who were working. In the meantime, the young men were energetically putting up a new house for the first chief of the district. They worked much more rapidly, and few sat around; in fact, very few at one time. They worked until dusk, and by then had completed the roof and half of the walls of the building. I spent the morning between these two jobs, taking pictures, listening, and observing. During the afternoon I wrote several letters to get them off on the boat that is expected tomorrow. Al and I are planning on taking this boat to Kayangle (an island to the north), stay overnight, and return Sunday, with Kai as our guide. Kai suggested it and it is a good opportunity for us.

November 8 In spite of the threat of rain and prospects of an unproductive trip, Kai and I went to Kayangle. Al decided to stay home. Our boat trip was more pleasant than I had expected. We did have a heavy sea for a distance of perhaps 10 miles just before reaching the Kayangle lagoon.

We arrived just after dark and were put up in a small vacant house, which probably is reserved for such occasions. A cot was brought for me and a mattress, mat, pillow, and blanket for both of us. We were brought food—fish, taro, and a kind of squash in coconut milk. After eating, Kai rather diffidently asked if I wanted to attend a dance. We went about 9:00 P.M. to an old building on the edge of the village. It apparently is a young people's recreation hall. Several boys and girls and also some young married men and women were there. A few of them danced in couples to some dismal records on an old phonograph. *Red Wing* was one of them. It was popular in the States when I was a teenager. I noticed that it was not unusual for two boys to dance together, even while girls sat around on the floor against the walls. I suppose this has been copied from our army personnel, because during the war there were soldiers stationed on the island.

After awhile Kai told a young man I would like to see one of the native women's dances called a *ngloik*. The women, and some boys on each end, lined up and, led by the young man standing in front of them, they sang and danced. The singing was in a confusion of languages including Palauan, Japanese, and English—very little of it entirely Palauan. There were a succession of dances and songs set off by intervals during which all of the dancers marked time, so to speak, with a relaxed forward kick, to a time count called by the leader who said: "Left, right, left, right,"—without regard to the named foot, however. This continued for perhaps one-half hour, after which they returned to the couple-type dancing. I asked Kai whether *ngloiks* were danced in Ulimang and he said no. Finally, he told me that the head chief of the district had prohibited them— which seems to account for the fact that several young people from Ulimang were on the same boat with us and attended the dance.

Men's clubhouse.

November 9 We were up early and walked around the southern end of the island. I saw an excellent specimen of the old-type canoe, placed under a well-constructed canoe shed, and a good, new rowboat. Also, I saw two old-style men's clubhouses, of which I obtained pictures. Our boat left for home at 9:30 A.M. but we did not arrive until 5:00 because of mechanical difficulties. Murphy reported that the young men's group had completed most of the work on the head chief's house by noon Saturday and then had a rather wild celebration—drunken arguments, threats with knives, and so forth. He thought that the anticipation of this was the reason why the head chief and Kai wanted to get us out of the village. This proved to be correct, because Kai came over about 9:00 P.M. and when the subject was raised he volunteered that he wanted to get us away from the village. He had seen an accumulation of liquor and expected trouble. He is getting rather confidential, and I think our trip to Kayangle broke some ice.

November 11 The second chief of Geklau invited me to visit him, saying that he would send a boat for me. I also had some small talk with a dynamic and sympathetic man of my age who lives near the Ngbuked men's clubhouse.

Interior of clubhouse.

He invited me to visit him, too. He speaks clearly and forcefully and is easier to understand than many others. I attribute some of this cordiality and other expressions of friendliness to my trip to Kayangle. It is my impression that this adventure served the purpose for which I had hoped, namely, to establish a closer bond between us and the ordinary people.

Kai came over in the late afternoon to put some bamboo shelving in our kitchen area. As usual the occasion turned out to be a language lesson. He is insisting, and rightly so, on my learning the vernacular as well as the more "classical" or stilted expressions found in dictionaries. With his acting ability and ingenuity these sessions are entertaining as well as instructive.

November 13   I was awakened about 3:00 A.M. because I was cold. I continued to doze until about 4:00, during which time the wind increased and the rain, which had begun about 10:00 P.M. last night, continued. By 4:30 there was a strong wind from the west, so much so that the curtain on our west window was flapping vigorously and the rain was coming in. By 5:00, Al and I were fully awake and concluded that we were in for a typhoon. We got up at 5:30, dressed, and prepared for breakfast. The wind and rain came in gusts. The violence reached a high point about 10:00 A.M. when a corner of our house lifted slightly off its foundation. We retreated to one part of one room to keep dry. Kai was busy nailing sheet iron covers over our windows and setting braces across our doors. By 11:00 his wife and others across the way became concerned about a heavy cluster of nuts swaying over our house. Kai and his brother-in-law came to tell us we had better go to the latter's house. We did, and sat there until 2:30 in the afternoon when I proposed to go home and eat. During this time there were several slack intervals, but no real abatement. There were strong gusts until 5:00 P.M., after which the storm began to subside, though it continued to rain until much later.

During the storm many young men made the village circuit—partly to help, partly out of excitement and curiosity. Considerable damage was done. Three coconut tree tops were broken off in our immediate vicinity. Many banana trees were blown down. Two houses in Ulimang collapsed; also one in Ngbuked, as well as the building at the end of the dock there.

November 21 I spent the morning sitting with and watching a group of older men building the new office. As always, there was an almost continuous stream of talk of one sort or another—everybody had something to say, everybody had some advice to give, everybody kibitzed. There was a lot of raillery and horseplay. All laughed at the jokes of others, and there were a lot of them.

November 23 This Sunday has been a very busy and a very long day. We started out at 10:30 in the morning with our cameras, intending to get some pictures for the record and at the same time to treat some of the people to pictures of themselves. We arrived at the Ngbuked men's clubhouse at 12:00, where the Protestant congregation was assembled. I supposed that the services were nearly over, so Al and I sat outside. Soon a boy was sent by the chief to ask us to come in; the services were just about to start. We stayed for them and afterwards took several pictures of members of the congregation. We continued our circuit of the district, finding almost every house closed.

December 1 Yesterday in talking with three of the older men I had several pertinent questions put to me: Why did the war occur; why did the Palauans get involved in it; why are we Americans here and not the Japanese; why do I want to study the Palauan people? These questions were asked in a perfectly friendly way. I felt rather helpless.

December 8 After watching activities around the store for a time, Al and I went to sketch the Ngbuked clubhouse. We spent the morning there but got little done because we became involved in a conversation with two men, one old and the other fairly young. The latter is a woodcarver who was taught his craft by the Japanese. He talked for some time about Japanese oppression. So did the old man. Both of them, like many others, seemed to delight in recounting the superior war exploits of the Americans over the Japanese. The old man excitedly described Palauan warfare, and also told us about the prostitutes who used to live in clubhouses with the young men.

December 11 Al and I returned to the Ngbuked clubhouse this morning to complete our sketching of it. We found that preparations were under way beside it for a turtle feast. The turtle was cooked by 11:00, so I had some of it at their invitation. Also some of the tapioca liquor which one of the men brought. I thought this was again an expression of their confidence in me because the making and the drinking of this liquor is forbidden by the administration.

December 17 The Catholic missionary who lives in Koror dropped in to see us unexpectedly at 4:30 this afternoon. He is making the rounds of the villages in preparation for Christmas services. He invited us to a prayer meeting and a children's catechism in the clubhouse here this evening. Both Al and I attended.

December 18 Just in the past few days I have noticed a change in the attitude of the people toward us. Or at least I think I do. Mingling as we have with them so regularly, they take us more for granted. They are less self-conscious, and there is no interruption in the proceedings, whatever they might be, when we arrive. No special attention is given to us. They are not so camera shy as they were in the beginning either—at least the men are not. The kids congregate around us as before but less out of curiosity than in friendliness.

December 19 The men from four of the villages of the district gathered at the Alap clubhouse to repair damages caused by the storm. All of them sewed nipa leaf patching, sitting in the shade on the platform in front of the clubhouse. Murphy sewed some too, which pleased the others. We came home at noon, and Al went back to work with the men and stayed until 4:30. He and I are invited to a completion feast tomorrow.

December 24 The blustery weather continued through the morning. I made a tour of the villages to check on activities, but was soon discouraged by the rain. I asked Kai if anything had been planned to celebrate Christmas and he said no, that a person had to go either to Koror or to Ngerchelong where there were to be services. Al and I have heard rumors, however, that native dances will be held here, either tomorrow or on New Year's. The Protestants are planning to go to Ngerchelong, and one of them asked me to accompany them. I refused, thinking that maybe something more interesting was going to be held here and that they were again trying to lure me away so I could not witness it. It now appears that I was wrong, but it is too late to switch, because I invited Kai to dinner tomorrow.

December 25 Kai appeared early, all dressed up, with his hair oiled and plastered down. He had promised to make noodles, which he had learned to do from the Japanese. He also wanted to watch our biscuit-making and other preparations. Instead, Rdor, his brother-in-law from across the path, brought noodles and stayed to watch and to help. Kai and I killed and plucked a chicken; Rdor cleaned it. The four of us had a gay time while dinner was being prepared—Al doing all the cooking. We were ready to eat by 3:00. Still I had seen nothing of Kai's wife, Emei, so I asked about her. She had gone to her taro field. It still did not occur to me that she was not to eat with us. It took a minute for me to grasp this—which I should have known, for Emei would not eat with Kai and me when I went to his house about 8:00 P.M. last Saturday before the family had eaten and was invited to stay for a meal. Emei and the children went in the other room and ate there. Families do not eat together when a guest is present, I know; but I thought that with this family it would be different.

December 27 It was a beautiful moonlit night and I could not go to sleep. I thought I heard singing in the distance. I fell asleep and awakened at 3:00 A.M. and again thought I heard music so I got up and walked along the beach. The tide was out, and the moon was high. It was just right for a dance and I believe that one was going but I could not locate it.

December 29 In the afternoon, beginning at 2:00, Al and I attended a district court session. Two of the village chiefs served as judges. There were four cases: A young man recently returned from Guam had beaten on a high-ranking man's door late at night; another man was charged with something that was not clear to me—and I am not certain it was clear to him either; three young school teachers were severely reprimanded for being drunk and showing off; and another man wanted to divorce his wife. This last case developed into a discussion between all concerned, and it was only secondarily a court case. It took a long time to argue that one through. Court was not over until 5:30.

January 1 Today Kai gave a dinner for Al and me. I had asked him to let me watch him cook it, but when I went to his house this morning at 9:30 everything was finished. Kai was not there. Emei said he was visiting. Their two girls, Doska and Iska, and their young son Azu were dressed in their finest— the girls wearing dresses that Emei had made from cloth that my wife sent for them.

Kai, his brother-in-law, Rdor, and one of his oil plant partners appeared about noon. They had planned that we were to eat outside so our tables were borrowed and set up under trees near the beach just back of our house. The men threw up a coconut leaf screen to hide us from the view of passers-by. It soon began to rain so we had to move into the house. Kai drew our blinds and closed our doors, the reason for the secrecy, I guessed, being that they did not want to be seen eating with us. The only other reason I could think of was that they did not want people seeing them giving us rum. Maybe they just wanted a private party, and knew that passing drunks would barge in; for as we were sitting many of them went by, yelling and staggering in an exaggerated fashion as they often do, and looking for any and everyone to call on. We kept very quiet until they had gone away. Finally, Rdor made a tentative gesture to eat—I judged to get Al and me started, for as it turned out they ate practically nothing. They left immediately after we had finished. I was disconcerted and even disgusted when I discovered that they lost no time eating the remains of the food which they took with them to Kai's house. I cannot explain this unless it is due to a reserve that is so deeply ingrained that they cannot shed it. There was nothing hostile in their behavior.

January 2 While Al and I were sitting on the bench at one corner of the schoolgrounds with Kai and two other men the "Crazy One" marched across the grounds and straight up to me. He took my feet, abruptly looked at the soles of my shoes, then briskly did the same with Al. Then he shouted at Al, accusing him of going around at night and doing something—it was not clear what. Then he went to the school building to tell the constable about it. We all took it hilariously. Later the constable came to apologize.

January 3 We went to Ngerchelong for a *kledaol*, which is a display of native dances and a feast. It was a two and one-half hour walk. There were several other Americans there, all of them officials and their wives who had come from Koror by boat. So was Reklai, the head chief of all the districts. After dinner with our compatriots I slipped away to a clubhouse on the outskirts of Ngerchelong where the young people were having fun. They were presenting skits and practicing the dances to be held tomorrow. I sat with Reklai in the front row, practically at the feet of the performers. I stayed until midnight, although Reklai repeatedly asked if I did not want to go to bed and apologized for the quality of the performances. It was just another example of their feeling that we cannot appreciate their inferior customs. I was determined not to leave, however, even if I did create an element of unease on their part.

January 12 The Ulimang head chief came by and invited me to his house at noon. I could not make out what the occasion was to be, and waited until a boy came to tell me that all was ready. By then I had seen all sorts of people going in the direction of his house carrying foods and pots, and I knew that a feast was going to be held. It still did not dawn on me that this was to be an *oraul*. While we were eating I noticed a plate being passed around and a man with a paper and pencil putting down the names of people who placed money in it. I asked the man next to me what this was about, and was told it was to help the chief pay for his new house. I then volunteered to contribute—to the astonishment of all—especially when I said $5. With that things began to perk up, and I was invited to go, right away, to another *oraul* in Ngbuked, to be given by one of the men who was sitting at our table. At 1:30 we started to walk to Ngbuked, which takes about one-half hour. I did not contribute to this man's *oraul*, because I could not see how I could gain by participating in all of these affairs and I could see how I could go broke. Anyway I ate again, a little, and sat around trying to understand the conversation until about 5:00 P.M.

January 14 I strolled to the schoolgrounds about 10:00 A.M. to see what was going on and found a meeting of some of the headmen and the young men's work group leaders in session. The discussion was about plans and work procedures, and also about food preparation for the coming *kledaol* on the 24th and 25th. This one is to be given in honor of the American administrative officials in Koror, along with the members of Pelelieu village, which is a kind of a brother community to Ulimang.

January 16 The women practiced their dances for the *kledaol* literally all night. They were singing when I woke up at 7:00 this morning. The men stopped at 10:00 last night. In going to practice they take bundles of goods— pillows, blankets, and food for their babies (which they also take with them) if not for themselves. The young people clearly object to so much work and the other demands on their time, but without any show of anger—in a joking way, but it is serious. Kai said there is too much work going on and no money coming in. He said that play on Saturday and Sunday is fine, but not dancing every night. Obviously the practicing is necessary because the people are no longer accustomed to dancing. They have to practice in order to put on a good show when the visitors arrive. They have to work at it because it is no longer fun.

January 26   After dinner Al and I went to the school where more dancing was to be held. The show started about 9:00. Al and I had front-center seats, along with the district chiefs and the head chief of Pelelieu. The dances of last night were repeated with more encores; and with different *shibais* presented. The latter were excellent amateur performances which the Palauans learned to stage from the Japanese. The evening was so cold that I could not stay for the finish. At 2:00 A.M. after one of the chiefs suggested that we could go if we felt like it, I left and went to bed. Al stayed along with the chiefs, until the party broke up, at 4:00 A.M.

January 27   As some of us were sitting around one corner of the schoolground waiting for a meeting with the chiefs to begin, the constable, who was among those assembled, explained that the cement monument in that corner was put up in 1928 to provide a niche for Tenuhega's (the Japanese Emperor) picture, and that every morning the school children had to bow toward it. The tree that stands nearby was planted at the same time. The constable talked much about events during the war, especially about American planes attacking. He also said that he thought it would be a good idea for the people of the district to plant a tree in memory of me, like the one for Tenuhega!

I wanted to see what was going on in other villages so I took the opportunity to give the carpenter who had worked on our house a good hammer. Kai noticed Al and I leaving our house and asked if he could go along. It turned out to be a very profitable trip. As we passed Tuman's house he came out to greet us. He was very talkative, and soon began to complain, or to explain, that all this business of the *kledaol* was "without purpose" and that most people dislike it. Kai agreed with him. They feel that the expense is too great, the work of providing food and of practicing dances is a waste of time and effort. It also leaves the Ngarard people broke. They said that the young people are timid and afraid to object to the older conservative ones because they would be called bad, unprincipled, and irresponsible. The young people look forward to the time when the oldsters die and their customs go with them.

January 29   I spent most of the morning at the school with Pelew. Daob, another teacher, listened to our conversation. He has been much more friendly during the past week, much more human than he usually is. It may have something to do with his putting more trust in us. The day after the *kledaol* I made a point of congratulating him on his performance in the *shibais* for two reasons: because they were very well acted, especially by him, and secondly to allay any anxiety he and others might have with respect to our witnessing the *shibais*. It was obvious that many people were uncertain how we were going to take two of them in particular: one displayed the Japanese flag, the other the beheading of two American airmen downed by the Japanese. At the time of the performances both the Ulimang and the Pelelieu chief made a point of explaining to me that all of this was just play-acting. Daob did the same, first to Al and later to me. Other people have taken the trouble to make the explanation, including the constable.

January 31   I went to the Alap clubhouse where I found an old man by the name of Aregon and another whose name I do not yet know. I talked with them—or they talked at me—for about two hours. They spoke of many things, mostly those occasioned by the presence here of the Americans, the Spanish, the Germans, and the Japanese. They recounted the now familiar stories about abuses by Japanese soldiers and the American war superiority; and as is always the case they laughed in telling about Japanese cruelty to them. I have never seen an expression of hatred on their faces. I did notice that Rdor showed sorrow when speaking of the death of his children due to Japanese negligence. I have encountered only head-shaking and joking about all of it even when they tell of the Japanese beating and robbing them.

I was told that soon an *oraul* would be held in the clubhouse here by a few chiefs to get money to pay the carpenter to put in the floor. And of course I was invited to attend. They also said they wanted to paint the inside of the clubhouse—with my paint, that is. Aregon told me briefly about the stories portrayed on a few of the beams of the clubhouse. He wants me to wait until his brother Tura comes back from Ngerchelong before we begin seriously writing down the stories that are pictured on the walls and facade of the clubhouse. He suggested that he and I go to another old clubhouse where the carvings are better preserved so he could show them to me, but I was getting hungry so I came home. On the way I again stopped to observe the man building the fish trap, and asked him to make a model for me.

Al walked to Ahol this afternoon. He wanted to see what goes on there on Saturdays, suspecting that young people go there to have their fun where they cannot be so easily observed by us. We have suspected that something or some things go on at night about which we are told nothing. Last night this end of the village was completely deserted as far as I could determine. No one was home, and there were no lights on in the houses. This is very unusual. We suspected some kind of a party in either Ngbuked or Alap. If it had not been so dark we would have taken a walk to explore late this evening, but it did not seem worthwhile especially because rain was threatening.

February 1   This morning at 10:00 Kai suggested that we go to the cemetery. Why, I am not quite sure, except that Emei wanted her picture taken there. We picked up her younger brother and a woman in another house who also wanted her picture taken. A noticeable attitude was their entirely secular behavior toward the graves and in their talk about the dead. There was no hush, no avoidance, no sentimental regard. I took pictures of the graves and head stones.

February 6 I paid a call on Ackul, "Mister Murphy's Friend." He has been busy trying to get a wife in Ngerchelong. He launched into this without prompting and told me the trouble that he is having. The woman or her people want too much money for her. However, he is going back tomorrow and thinks that a bargain can be made. He said he would bring his wife to see us.

Just in the past month I have noticed a decided improvement in my mastery of this language. Until recently it has been mostly disconnected words, but now I can build and understand sentences. The striking thing about this is the suddenness with which it has happened. Secretly I had almost given up hope that I would ever be able to learn to really *speak* the language, although I did understand it fairly well.

February 10 I went in search of Sakau, wanting a haircut. His shop is in his home. He sent his son to get two green coconuts so that we could have a refreshing drink. In the meantime he carefully washed all his accessories. He gave me a good haircut and razor trim—all around the eyes, including my eyebrows, the temple hairline, and up my nose. It was undoubtedly the most thorough haircut I ever had. His razor was quite dull and he damned it as Japanese, and of course praised one of American manufacture that he had seen in Koror. He talked quite a bit, mostly dissatisfied talk about community work still to come, but also about Palauan customs which encourage wealth differences between the people.

February 17 For several days I have been hinting to Nira, the second chief of our district, that I would like to accompany a party of Ulimang people due to go to Ahol to negotiate a financial settlement occasioned by the death of the wife of a chief of that village. He has been noncommittal until around noon today when he sent word that we would leave in a couple of hours. Upon arrival in Ahol our party went directly to the clubhouse. No one was there at the time, but a boy was sent by Nira for Mega, the deceased woman's husband. He came immediately and Nira apologized for having arrived a day in advance of schedule, explaining that I wished to see what was to go on and that I wanted to stay overnight. They talked about this for awhile, then Mega excused himself saying that he had many things to attend to. A few other men appeared by the time darkness fell, including several from Ulimang. I took a walk to see what was going on and to get a little relaxation, returning about dusk. Soon after that food was brought to us on individual trays. In the meantime women arrived and their children seated themselves at the opposite end of the clubhouse from the men. They were served food, and slept in the clubhouse, as we did, that night.

There was much talk after dinner and we finally settled into our bedding about midnight. Four kerosene lamps hung down the middle of the clubhouse, and they remained lighted all night. The sleepers began to arise at daybreak. I was among the last, getting up about 6:30. This, again, is an example of how little these people sleep during the night. They do take naps during the daytime, but they often sleep only a few hours at night.

February 18 Rash, one of the Ngbuked chiefs, suggested that he and I look for water to wash our faces, so we went to the bathing spot some distance away. He bathed, I just washed. The rest of the people evidently did not even get wet. Since I knew it would be some time before breakfast I took my tin cup, some Nescafe, and canned heat tablets out of my bag and went to the beach to make coffee for myself. I walked down the beach to a place where a turtle was being cut up for the feast, but I was not very hospitably received, so I went back through the village to the clubhouse. I arrived there about 9:00 to find that food was being served and others were waiting for me. That was the beginning of a very long day, most of it spent in a cramped sitting position listening to hours of low-keyed talk about who owed whom what.

February 20 Aleman, a chief of Ngbuked, dropped by this morning, bringing four eggs, and obviously seeking cigarettes. I gave him a package, and then hinted that I would be very pleased to have the broken bead of Palauan money that he showed me last Sunday. He gladly gave it to me, taking it out of his handbag, and even volunteered to look for a better piece. He was reluctant only to let me have the *broken* one. He wants to have a whole piece taken to the States. Asked the value of this bead, he said that if it were whole it would be worth about $30; in Japanese times perhaps $50. It can be perforated, can still be used to buy goods, but it would be worth perhaps only a few dollars among Palauans.

I wrote notes after Aleman left for a couple of hours and then I decided to make the circuit through the villages with the ultimate objective of seeing Nira. I wanted to appeal to him to let me know when things such as funerals are going to happen. It has been rather aggravating that, in accordance with native protocol, no one but a chief informs us of what is going on or what is expected to occur that is out of the ordinary.

I also stopped at the house of Saig to see the new baby. She is seventeen days old and is the one that I more or less named at Saig's request. I chose the name Jane because it is relatively easy for Palauans to pronounce.

February 22 Masas did not appear for instruction in English today, as I had hoped he would not, and I spent the day alone. It gave me an opportunity to collect my thoughts about the information I have been getting on clans and property, and to formulate some questions about it. After dinner I went over to Kai's house and we had another session about it. Now that I have the general idea and know some of the kinship terms, I am making headway, but many details remain to be cleared up. It is a very complicated situation.

February 25 I went in search of Nira this morning. He had previously asked me if I had any tar patching for the nail holes in his tin roof. It happened that I had, so I took a can of it to him. He was grateful and invited me to have lunch. While this was being prepared I again told him that I would like very much to know when something important was planned. I explained that I was attempting to write the "truth" about Palauan customs to take back to America, and that in order to do this I wanted to see things for myself and not depend on rumors and "lies." He was genuinely sympathetic, but said that some occasions, such as a funeral, were private family matters, and that only members of the family could invite outsiders, and even then only the family heads really have this privilege.

February 27 I visited Rash this morning to give him the same pep talk that I gave to Nira about advising me and inviting me to parties and ceremonies —after thanking him for the trip to Ahol. He too seemed agreeable, but did not elaborate his answer as much as Nira did. He asked if I had been to an *oraul* (forgetting that I had gone to two of them with him). I think he had in mind that one was even at that moment just about to start in the little hamlet of Kale, which is just a few minutes' walk from here. I told him that I would like to get some genealogies from him. He agreed, saying that we could do it next Sunday. Then he began to explain about the ratings of Ngbuked families. Aleman joined us and we had some light talk about old customs. Soon Aleman left, saying he was going to Kale. When I asked why, he said that he had "some business" over there. "Some business!"

I should be more patient with these people, at least as patient as they are with me. They have been very generous with their time, and have invited me to participate with them in most of their group activities. In spite of my undeniable charm and tact, I must nonetheless be a nuisance at times, and only their good nature prevents them from expressing irritation with my incessant prying into their private affairs.

March 6 I returned from Koror with Goss, a government official. He was going to Nemat to supervise the election of a new chief there, and he invited me to go with him. We arrived about 8:30 P.M. and were taken to the clubhouse, where two cots with mosquito nets were already set up for Goss and myself; bedrolls and mats were brought for the rest of the party. The election was to take place the next day, Sunday, so there was nothing to do but talk. We all went to bed about 12:00, but the gnats were so bad that most of the Palauans left the clubhouse and went to the beach where they built smudges.

March 7 We were up early, in fact shortly after daybreak, for Goss had to catch the boat at 1:00. After breakfast the election was held—if it can be called that. Under the direction of Goss all the externals of a secret ballot were there, but the proceedings were an obvious farce because the outcome had been predetermined by the Palauan style of behind-the-scenes political maneuvering, the basic features of which are not confined to the Palauan islands. Goss was dejected and not a little annoyed.

March 10 This morning I passed the home of Saig, whose wife had a baby on February 6. She was sitting in the doorway with nothing on but her pants, and was not at all embarrassed when I asked her how the baby was. She is the first woman who has not tried hastily to cover her upper body when Al or I appear. She was just as casual the other time I stopped to see the baby, though then she was partly covered with a ragged dress. Most women are embarrassed even to nurse children in my presence. Emei has several times hastily taken her breast from her baby when I have unexpectedly appeared. A few women on the Koror boat have gone ahead with their nursing in a half-concealed way when I have been near them in the cabin.

March 13 Emei told me this morning that Risa, an elderly woman of about sixty, came to her home last night and waited for me so she could tell me about old Palauan birth customs. Emei had asked her to do this. A little later I met Risa on the path in front of our house and we set a time for me to go to her house tonight. She talked freely and easily. She, like many others, knows about Kubary (a German ethnologist) and praises his knowledge of Palauan language and customs. She knows a few German words herself she said, and then proceeded to sing *The Kaiser is a Good Man*—to the tune of *God Save the King*.

March 16 About 7:00 this evening Risa came to see me and whispered that a young woman living nearby had given birth, but that the placenta had failed to appear. She had been sent by the chiefs to see if I could help. I put two aspirin tablets in my pocket and followed her to a small house in one room of which the sick woman lay with several older women sitting close by. The other room was crowded with men. The sick woman had a headache and a slight fever, so I offered the tablets saying that there was nothing else that I could do. Some of those present were obviously skeptical. I found it almost impossible to explain to them that although I am a "doctor" I really am not.

March 19 The women's work group cleared the trails to the cemetery and around the clubhouse. I approached them with my movie camera and asked if I could take pictures of them at work. I was agreeably surprised, for they were quite willing, only showing embarrassment about stooping over with their backsides to the camera. Risa was especially helpful, and even made an old-fashioned hat of banana leaves, such as women used to wear in the fields, and put it on for my benefit. Many of the women sang as they worked. I was with them for an hour or more, after which I came back to the clubhouse and talked with three old women for awhile. They too were very friendly. One of them asked if I could get some dye for her graying hair. She explained that the Japanese women dyed their hair and that the Palauan women copy them.

March 22 I scarcely got out of my chair today from 8:30 in the morning until 2:00 this afternoon. While I was still writing notes after breakfast, Tura dropped in. He wanted a pair of spectacles. Last week I gave a pair to Rdor. (I brought fifteen pairs, having bought them at Woolworth's before I left.) The word that I have them spread rapidly. Several of the people really need glasses and this is the only way they can get them. I pumped Tura for an hour, and when his brother arrived I began on him. Soon another man showed up. I steered the talk to religion and Tura told some myths and described shamanistic practices. He shied away from contemporary religious beliefs. When this seemed to end in an impasse we turned to family histories and to kinship terminology.

March 26 About 9:00 A.M. I took Risa a package of cigarettes in return for a fish she brought me last night. She told me a child had died earlier in the morning in Alap. This was sudden news to me, so I got busy and asked the child's relatives if I could attend the funeral. All said that it would be O.K. I went to Alap with several of them around 10:00, and spent the rest of the day watching the funeral rites. Later I questioned Emei and Risa about what I had seen and about the relationships of the child to the people who were present.

April 8 Tura stuck his head in our doorway early this morning. He had been "on business" to Kale, and was hotfooting it to Ngerchelong. I am sure by now that he is an active member of *modekne* (a nativistic cult that was suppressed by the Japanese and is at present actively discouraged by the American health authorities). He seems forever to be going around the island visiting people. He and the old man who was with him warmed to my attempts to talk about Palauan religion, and I think Tura is about ready to tell me more about his "business." He said he would be back to see me on Saturday.

April 12 Rash called on me and stayed for an hour. I gave him a cigarette lighter, and questioned him about the elaborate ceremony for the woman and her newborn that has been going on for the last four days. He said that it was the "real Palauan way," but that few families follow the custom today. He added that the full treatment given this woman was mainly because the people wanted me to see it and that Nira had urged that it be done. I think, however, that Risa was the real mainspring.

Ackul came by early this morning to say that he had come from Niwal, that the money for the marriage of his daughter there was ready, and that he must now get food together for the feast. I am going to Niwal with him. He says "the business part" of the marriage ceremony will take place on Thursday. He was on his way to Geklau to buy coconuts, betel, and other feast goods. Plans for his own marriage are stalled. He thinks the woman and her relatives are just "playing with" him.

April 17 I was sick with dysentery for the three days I was in Niwal with Ackul, and did not do much besides watch the marriage proceedings. We were supposed to leave last night but no boat was available. I was fed up with the place, and with fish, and wanted to come home, but went to bed early, as I did every night, and waited for this morning. We were supposed to leave at dawn, but still no boat was available, and the hours dragged on. Finally, Ackul borrowed a canoe with an out-rigger and the five in our party from Ulimang boarded it for home.

April 22 This evening I walked through the villages. It was a beautiful night with a full moon. Many people work on nights like this. Women were carrying baskets of taro from their plots to Alap. Torong was sewing roof thatching by a dim light. I stayed for awhile with him and a man who was visiting him. They wanted to know about the American school system. We talked, as I have so often with almost all of the older people, about the Negroes in America. I also had the pleasure of hearing Torong explain to his friend why they are black and why Al and I are white—the biblical story.

April 29 I decided to make a frontal attack on the *modekne* business, so I went to Nira's house with a little gift for his wife. Esube, another high-ranking man, was there, as was Nira's adopted son. At what I thought was the proper moment I told Nira that I would like to attend a meeting of the *modekne*. The request startled both of the older men, but after the first shock they said I could not attend a meeting because none are being held, but maybe I could talk with someone, whereupon Nira called his son to his side and whispered to him. The boy left and soon returned with word that it would be O.K. When did I want to talk? I said this afternoon. The name of the informant was not mentioned, but I guessed that it was Tura, and this turned out to be right. Nira took me to the clubhouse where Tura was waiting alone. Having sanctioned our meeting, Nira left. Tura was quite willing to talk, but very hush-hush. He spoke so quietly that I could hardly hear him at times. He is a firm believer in the cult, and he gave me a subjective account of it, mentioning only those features he knew I would approve of. It was nonetheless a most informative session, filling the gaps in what I already knew about the cult.

May 3 I found Kai in an informative mood, and plied him with questions on land inheritance and related subjects. He was interested in the map of plot ownership that I had drawn up. He supplemented it with corrections of the boundaries in a way that indicated to me that he knew what he was doing. He said he knew about these lands and their ownership because he has bought coconuts from the owners.

May 9 We were invited to Masas' home for a meal. It was one of the farewell variety and came at an odd hour for us. We were invited at 10:00 A.M. "to talk and visit." Food was served soon after we arrived, and there was a great quantity of it. Masas wrapped the remains of our meal in banana leaves and took them to our house. It would have been undignified for us to carry them.

May 10 We were invited to another "little dinner" at noon in the house of Kari. I must say that this meal was the worst that I have encountered—five boiled eggs, all of them so rancid that they could not be hard-boiled, along with some boiled taro. I did my best with it. I also tasted some *wassa*, which is the salted, boiled-down essence of fish. I have often seen the stuff but had not eaten any. It looks like axle grease, and it must taste worse.

May 12 We were invited to another festivity at 4:00 P.M., this time a feast given by Saig in celebration of the birth of his daughter, Jane. We again had lots of food, altogether too much; but all of us have thought that Al and I would be leaving the day after tomorrow. This morning our travel orders arrived, and the date of our departure is now set for May 21. This gives us some needed time, but it is anticlimactic.

May 18   It is becoming more difficult by the day to get anything but snatches of information, here and there. All have our departure on their minds and they inevitably direct discussions to that subject. They want to know about our proposed trip, and then about America. They thereby turn the tables on me, and I become the informant. As a consequence of this and various other things, including farewell dinners, this week has been enjoyable but not very productive. . . .

Epilogue

Shortly after Murphy and I completed our research in Palau I wrote a monograph which I called *Palauan Society: A Study of Contemporary Native Life in the Palau Islands.* It had a dual purpose. One was to provide information for the guidance of American officials whose responsibility it was to administer the affairs of the island population as a whole. This was an important but not an overriding consideration, because the Office of Naval Research, through the National Academy of Sciences, had sponsored, partially financed, and materially facilitated our research for whatever practical benefit the administrative officials could derive from it. Our observations and inquiries were not specified or controlled by the Navy. From the outset it was understood that they were to be in the nature of "pure" research. In consequence, *Palauan Society* could serve its second purpose, which was "to fill the gap in our scientific knowledge of the area that was closed to investigation for many years by the Japanese" (Preface, p. iii). In other words, it was intended to be an ethnographic account comparable to hundreds of others written by anthropologists describing other ethnic groups, primarily for fellow members of their profession. It is objective and analytical. In it Palauan custom is identified and described in ways that are customary among anthropologists. Things, beliefs, and behaviors were selected and assigned to such standardized conceptual realms as subsistence, kinship, religion, birth, marriage, and death. The data presented in this systematic fashion were drawn almost entirely from the impersonal record of numerous observations and responses to inquiries contained in my notebooks by the usual method of classifying, indexing, interrelating, and generalizing from them.

As well as can be determined, *Palauan Society* has served its purposes adequately, though not beyond the degree expected. Yet even at the time of writing it I knew that a good half of the picture of Palauan life was missing for the practical-minded administrator as well as for the anthropological theorist. In common with other books of its kind it lacks vitality. It does not tell the reader what it means to live like a Palauan. It does not present his view of what anthropologists call his culture, or how he lives by or with it. It gives only glimpses of a commonplace observation in Ulimang; namely, that Palauans usually live according to the rules of custom because it is to their advantage to do so, but with the ever-present temptation to either break them or manipulate them to satisfy their personal needs and ambitions, just as Americans and every other people do; and that conformance is characterized by individual variations about a norm that may or may not be explicit, just as it is elsewhere. It is this dimension of understanding the Palauans which is recorded, however sketchily, in the Journal. The microscopic detail in that record is the analogue of the macroscopic forms and categories that were abstracted and summarized from my notebooks. In it I endeavored to describe to myself how it felt to try to live and think like a Palauan, as well as what it meant to them personally insofar as I could ascertain this by the means indicated in the excerpts above.

Being a Palauan is very much a product of the Journal, and is thus an analogue of *Palauan Society*. As is stated in its Introduction (p. 3),

An effort has been made throughout to convey an understanding of Palauan society and culture by presenting the Palauan view of the world in terms of the author's understanding of how the Palauan sees and comprehends what goes on around him. The objective, then, has been to delineate a way of life as free from the anthropologist's conventionalized structuring of it as possible, in the hope of communicating what it means to live and die in a small village in Palau.

It is egocentric. It attempts to depict the individual's apperception of the Palauan universe; his confrontation and interaction with things and people as he conceives them to be; his comprehension of and behavior with respect to what we call accidents, typhoons, Americans, births, deaths, his father, his foster father, his elders, his chief, his gods, and his soul. The orientation and emphasis is on being and doing, on the continuity of events and personalities over time and as they interact at the moment.

Anthropologists have spent a great deal of time, especially since 1950, arguing about which of these approaches is "real," valid, or most productive. At present the argument often takes the form of an opposition between what are termed the "emic" and the "etic" interpretations, the "insider's" versus the "outsider's" view, based upon the distinction in linguistic analysis between phonemes and phonetics. In my opinion neither of these interpretations is adequate by itself to enable us to understand a people or to explain their behaviors. Moreover, they cannot be cleanly separated. They overlap and interpenetrate, and where they do not they are complementary. Sometimes a skillful ethnographer can weave them into the fabric of one description, but it is not easy and usually not professionally acceptable. The alternative, given the desire on the part of the ethnologist, is to present the two dimensions separately and to link them, knowing fully well that neither can be completely divorced from the other. This is why I welcomed the opportunity to write *Being a Palauan*, and now to relate it to *Palauan Society* and to the personal encounters with Palauan beliefs and behaviors that are recorded in the Journal.

The case study is not, and should not be as personal as is the Journal. Still, they are comparable in tone and orientation, and there are deliberate linkages between them. The opening paragraphs of the case study, for example, describe one of the many tantrums of Azu, who is the same little boy mentioned by that name in the Journal, and one of whose fits of temper I recorded on motion picture film as well as in deleted portions of the Journal. Similarly for the frequent references to his father and mother, Kai and Emei, whom I regarded not only as good friends but as voluntary research assistants. In fact, my intimate acquaintance with this family, and the entrée into the community which it provided, convinced me that I could and should write something like *Being a Palauan*. Kai spoke of me to others as his elder brother. He treated me as such and I was so accepted by other residents of Ngarard. This was neither as false nor as difficult as it might be in other societies because the establishment of fictive kinships is a Palauan custom. It gave me a place in their social system, in addition to the one I inevitably was assigned as a prestigious outsider and a privileged associate of their chiefs. In both roles I was something of a showpiece, especially after I learned to speak the language fairly well and (unwittingly) used "big" words—those found in German-Palauan dictionaries and habitually used only by elderly men. In true Palauan style the people of our district delighted in exhibiting me to visitors from elsewhere, beaming when I spoke to them as if to say "See what *we* have!" Above all, what convinced me that I knew the Palauans well enough to write the case study was that I learned to appreciate and engage their sense of humor. It is often said that this is one of the most esoteric and elusive aspects of any people's culture. There is evidence enough in the Journal that the Palauans like to joke, and some indications that they often do it about events and circumstances which many Americans would regard as misfortunes to oneself or to others. It may be added that much of their humor would be considered to be banal, contrived, crass, or childish by many Americans. The point is that if one gets to know them well enough, it turns out that many Palauans feel the same way about the merriment of some of their countrymen. In other words Palauans, like Americans, are comically as well as socially stratified.

It would be misleading to leave the impression that I believe I became a Palauan. That would have been impossible even if I had cherished the hope. It is obvious in several of the Journal excerpts—and it is intended to be—that there were areas of belief and behavior to which I remained a stranger and others about which I learned only through an aggressive suspicion. The most that can be claimed is that I temporarily and moderately successfully straddled two ways of life.

Like many other ethnographic accounts, neither *Palauan Society* nor *Being a Palauan* has much to say about how the data for them were collected. Although it should not be so, anthropologists generally expect their colleagues to take their field methods for granted; and it is true that most procedures in data collection are so well known and routinized that professional readers do, rightly or wrongly, expect that they have been employed. The same readers will readily recognize research strategies and techniques in the excerpts from the Journal—

among them what are commonly referred to as gaining entree, identification of purpose, establishment of rapport, the use of key informants, surveying or cross-sectioning the universe of custom, role-playing, the repetition of observations and queries, and genealogical charting. These techniques and others are implicit in the excerpts above. In fact, the latter were selected for that reason. Other contributors to this volume on method will no doubt formally present and illustrate some of them by reference to their own case studies. It might be worthwhile for the nonprofessional reader to reverse this tactic and to identify the methods that are embodied in relevant excerpts from the Journal.

It should not be overlooked that keeping a journal is itself a research device which may be variously employed or not employed at all. Some ethnologists make of it an impersonal record of daily events comparable to a ship's log. It is evident that for me *Palauan Journal* was something more. It was a means of regularly thinking over each day's events and planning for those ahead. It thus provided a subjective measure of accomplishment. But it was also a therapeutic device which enabled me to systematically talk to myself, to quietly explode, and to privately confess my frustrations, anxieties, and failures.

The Journal ends abruptly, in the original as in the last excerpt. This is a reflection of the state of the research as well as my state of mind. I left Ulimang knowing that the investigation was incomplete and that it was likely to remain so. No group study ever has an end as long as the group exists because it is always changing, especially in the modern world. Being a Palauan today is not the same life experience that it was in 1948. Partly for this reason and partly for others, some of the younger Americanized generation have expressed doubts that it ever was what it seemed to me twenty years ago. Admitting that there is always some justification for such disagreement, and anticipating that it will be expressed by people who read what is written about them, is part of being an anthropologist.

Recommended Reading

BARNETT, H. G., 1949, *Palauan Society*. Eugene, Oregon: University of Oregon Press.

A report on Palauan life as of 1948 with attention also given to customs which antedate contacts with Europeans, Japanese, and Americans.

————, 1956, *Anthropology in Administration*. Evanston, Ill.: Row, Peterson.

A review of the uses of anthropological knowledge in the administration of native peoples, the major part of which is devoted to American Micronesia and its problems under changing conditions.

KEESING, F., 1946, *The South Seas in the Modern World*. New York: John Day.

A survey which the author says "attempts to define comprehensively the political, strategic, and economic role these Oceanic islands play in the world today, and especially the modern experience and problems of the peoples native to them."

MAHONEY, FRANCIS B., 1950, *Projective Psychological Findings in Palau Personality*. Unpublished Master's Thesis, University of Chicago.

A probing of unconscious motivations and attitudes using TAT and Rorschach cards. The results, combined with observed behavior, yield the interpretation presented in Chapter 2 of this book.

MEAD, MARGARET, 1930, *Growing Up in New Guinea*. Blue Ribbon Books.

An intimate study of the socialization process among the Manus, a people living on an island to the southeast of Palau. Some of their customs, especially those revolving around wealth and marriage, strikingly resemble those of Palau.

OLIVER, DOUGLAS L., 1946, *Planning Micronesia's Future. A Summary of the U.S. Commercial Company's Economic Survey of Micronesia.* Cambridge, Mass.: Harvard University Press.

Regional studies by a team of scientists, including anthropologists, for the purpose of assessing island resources and their relation to island culture.

————, 1951, *The Pacific Islands.* Cambridge, Mass.: Harvard University Press. A treatment of all the islands, the bulk of which is devoted to changes in historic times. References to Micronesia occur throughout.

RITZENTHALER, ROBERT E., 1954, *Native Money of Palau.* Milwaukee Public Museum, Publications in Anthropology, No. 1.

A detailed description of types of men's money with sections on their use, acquisition, value, and relation to the altered economy of the islands due to foreign contacts.

ROBSON, R. W., *The Pacific Islands Handbook, 1944* (and succeeding years). New York: Macmillan.

A compilation of a variety of data, including brief descriptions of the physical aspects of the islands, their resources, populations, histories, administrations, and facilities.

U. S. NAVY DEPARTMENT, Office of Chief of Naval Operations, 1948, *Handbook on the Trust Territory of the Pacific Islands.*

A comprehensive report on American Micronesia with emphasis on conditions subsequent to World War II, but containing brief descriptions of the pre-European cultures of the different island groups.

VIDICH, ARTHUR J., 1949, *Political Factionalism in Palau.* Mimeographed report.

Clan structure, kinship, religion, rank, warfare, and economy are shown to be involved in the factionalism resulting from foreign contacts.